Collector's Encyclopedia
of
AMERICAN
FURNITURE

Volume 1

The Dark Woods of the Nineteenth Century
Cherry, Mahogany, Rosewood and Walnut

Robert W. and Harriett Swedberg

COLLECTOR BOOKS
A Division of Schroeder Publishing Co., Inc.

The current values in this book should be used only as a guide. They are not intended to set prices, which vary from one section of the country to another. Auction prices as well as dealer prices vary greatly and are affected by condition as well as demand. Neither the Authors nor the Publisher assumes responsibility for any losses that might be incurred as a result of consulting this guide.

Additional copies of this book may be ordered from:

Collector Books
P.O. Box 3009
Paducah, KY 42002-3009

@ $24.95 – Add $2.00 for postage and handling.

Copyright: Robert W. and Harriett Swedberg, 1991

Other Books By Robert W. and Harriett Swedberg

American Clocks and Clockmakers

American Oak Furniture Styles and Prices, revised edition

American Oak Furniture Styles and Prices, Book II

American Oak Furniture Styles and Prices, Book III

Antiquing in England: A Guide to Antique Centres

Country Furniture and Accessories with Prices

Country Furniture and Accessories with Prices, Book II

Country Furniture Styles and Prices, revised edition

Country Store 'N More

Furniture of the Depression Era

Off Your Rocker

Tins 'N Bins

Victorian Furniture Styles and Prices, revised edition

Victorian Furniture Styles and Prices, Book II

Victorian Furniture Styles and Prices, Book III

Wicker Furniture Styles and Prices, revised edition

ACKNOWLEDGMENTS

Since we do not use photographs from museums in our books, extensive traveling is required in order to obtain illustrations. Many private homes and shops were visited in each of the ten states listed. We are humbly grateful to all the people who spent many hours with us and helped us move furniture in order to obtain the best shots possible. We also appreciated the aid of those who did not choose to be acknowledged but who likewise assisted us. Thank you - one and all - for providing us with special photographs for this book. They will help to educate others who are seeking to learn more about the furniture available to Victorian Era American home-makers of the 1800's.

ANTIQUE AMERICA
Norman, Lance and Cheryle Frye
Davenport, Iowa

ANTIQUES AT OUR HOUSE
Dick and Bernie King
Minneapolis, Minnesota

BEFORE OUR TIME
Dave and Betty Mallory
Morton, Illinois

BOB'S ANTIQUES
Bob M. DeBerry
Whitewright, Texas

LARRY AND SANDY BOLTZ

BURLINGTON ARCADE ANTIQUE MALL
Lincoln, Nebraska

ERIC AND STACEY CARTER AND KYLE

ROBERT AND LUCILE CARTER

ROGER CARTER

RONNIE CARTER

JIM AND GWEN ESTILL

LYN AND JAN GALLUP

REV. AND MRS. E.W. HANCOCK

MONA AND MARC KLARMAN

LAND OF LINCOLN ANTIQUES
(AND SPECIALTIES) MALL
Rockford, Illinois

THE LOUISVILLE ANTIQUE MALL
Harold L., Chuck and Don Sego
Louisville, Kentucky

FERN AND BILL LYON

SAM AND LAWANNA McCLURE

MURPHY'S ANTIQUES
Pat and Patsy
Whitewright, Texas

ODDS 'N ENDS ANTIQUES
Wayne and Lila Hale
Vandalia, Illinois

OLD EVANSVILLE ANTIQUE MALL
Mr. and Mrs. Ed Small
Evansville, Indiana

REALTY AND AUCTION SERVICE
John A. Whalen
Neapolis, Ohio

DALE AND VERONICA RUPP

DOUG AND NANCY RUPP

SCHOOL DAYS MALL
Judy and Eric Sewell
Sturtevant, Wisconsin

CLARK AND JEAN SHANNON
Milwaukee, Wisconsin

BILL AND NANCY THURSTON

BONNIE AND DENTON TUSSING

INTRODUCTION

The prices of the furniture listed in this book were set by the dealers and collectors who own the pieces pictured. This "price tag" policy is followed in the many other books written by Robert W. and Harriett Swedberg. *The values listed are to serve as a guide only and neither the authors nor the publisher assumes responsibility for any losses that may be incurred as a result of using this book.*

It is not possible to declare emphatically that a specific maker created an item of furniture unless it bears the original label or a bill of sale is available. Otherwise, a qualifying statement is proper, such as "attributed to John Belter," "in the Jelliff manner," "reminiscent of Meeks," "in the Roux style" or "with Mallard characteristics." Authentic catalogues or price lists with illustrations, family legends with possible lore added through the years or photographs that include passe furniture can help identify pieces. Known examples of a craftsman's work provide a comparison for the scholar. For example, some of Belter's chairs with rose and grape carvings on their crest were named for the Natchez, Mississippi home, Rosalie, for which they were purchased, about 1859 or 1860, just prior to the Civil War. They remain on display there, and other Rosalie chairs with variations were also produced.

This book deals with American furniture made from the dark woods used in the 1800's, mainly mahogany, rosewood, walnut, and cherry. Its focus is on the Empire and Victorian styles. Collectors and dealers realize that furniture cannot all be put into a precise time frame. There is an overlapping when one style wanes and another becomes dominant. Thus, the two run concurrently for a matter of years. Because of this, circa (about) becomes a helpful word. Since various furniture types might exist for a twenty to thirty year time span, it is possible to say circa to indicate that a piece could have been created a few years prior to or a few years after the date stated. A definition of the Empire and Victorian Era is necessary. Both periods were named for European heads of state.

Emperor Napoleon Bonaparte was in and out of power in France for sixteen years (1799-1815). He demanded furniture that depicted his image and designers catered to him by borrowing from ancient Egypt, Greece and Rome to create the Empire style named for him. Massive, masculine, ornate, highly ornamented furniture resulted. It was popular in France from about 1805-1820. It influenced American cabinet-makers, who usually produced more subdued examples, from 1810-1840.

Transitional pieces represent a combination of designs from the out-going style to the new. Therefore, a sofa with the new Victorian feel might have a curved back and legs but the apron could appear heavy and straight. The Empire favored straight lines and rectangular shapes. Early Victorian forms were curved.

Her Majesty Queen Victoria ruled the British Empire for 63 years. Because of this, it is a mistake to assume that the furniture created during her reign from 1837 to 1901 all looked alike. Styles changed. By the 1850's, overpowering rectilinear lines were developing. There were also various forms developed that had a country feel or did not remain in production too long. It is convenient to lump all the furniture made during Queen Victoria's reign as Victorian furniture, but it does not all fit under one category. A furniture chart follows to help show some of the influences that prevailed. Remember, the Industrial Revolution brought a change from objects being made with hand tools by craftsmen to the making of furniture in factories by machine. This switch to mass production was another factor during the Victorian Era. A chart giving approximate dates with an indication of the types of dark wood furniture (mahogany, walnut, rosewood and cherry) follows. Even though there is an overlapping, as has already been stated, the general age specifications considered will be the early, middle, and late 1800's.

MAIN CHARACTERISTICS
OF DARK WOOD FURNITURE OF THE 1800's

Early Century
Age of Mahogany

American Empire (circa 1810-1840) - Age of mahogany with some rosewood and ebony also.
- Ponderous lines with symmetical, rectangular shapes
- Mainly crafted by hand
- Thick lyre bases and scrolls
- Acanthus leaf and laurel branch swags
- Wings as feet on sofas
- Ogee frames
- Beading
- Cornices on secretaries and cupboards
- Round wooden pulls or lion head back plates with ring pulls for handles
- French Emperor influence felt

Middle Century
Age of Victorian Walnut

Gothic (circa 1820-1850) overlaps with early century. Not much was made.
- Church look
- Pointed spires resembling old-fashioned church steeple
- Rounded arches
- Light appearance
- Tracery resembling cathedral windows

Louis XV Revival (circa 1840-1865). Imitated original Louis XV style (French king, 1715-1774), but not as ornate.
- Straight lines avoided
- Curves essential
- Feminine look in furniture
- Elliptical shapes rather than round
- Rococo carvings (rock, shell, flowers, animals)
- Marble tops
- Fancy leaf, fruit and nut carved handles

- Cabriole legs
- Finger roll frames
- Walnut with some rosewood and mahogany

Renaissance (circa 1850-1885) overlaps with late century
- Extravagant, tall furniture
- High bedsteads, secretary desks, and cabinets
- Machine made, frequently with hand-carved details
- Carved crests and pediments
- Roundels
- Carved wooden pulls
- Ebony and gilt handles (now called tear drops)
- Cluttered pedestal bases on tables
- Turned finials
- Urns
- Carved heads of leaders such as George Washington or Columbia (a woman symbolizing the United States) created to celebrate the nation's centennial in 1876
- Marble tops
- Walnut

Late Century
Age of Victorian Walnut

Eastlake (circa 1870-1890). England's furniture maker Charles Locke Eastlake's influence felt.
- Rectangular
- Straight, clean lines
- Desired well-made furniture, not cheaply cluttered machine-made products.
- Incised lines
- Parallel continuous incised lines now called railroad tracks
- Chip carving
- United States added appendages to clutter Eastlake's simple look

Encylopedia Listings
of
AMERICAN FURNITURE

ARMOIRE (or Wardrobe)

Originally an armoire was a Middle Age's storage unit for armor. Now it is a sophisticated term for its descendent, the wardrobe, a tall cupboard in which clothes are hung. Some include drawers.

Walnut armoire or wardrobe, two pieces, with applied decorations and ring molding, 42" wide, 18½" deep, 87" high, Middle Century.

B

BANQUET TABLE

Before extension tables were developed, tables of the same height would be joined together to form one large dining unit. A center table with its two drop leaves raised was united with two console tables that flanked the walls when not in use. Their leaves could be extended also.

Mahogany and mahogany veneer Empire banquet table in two pieces, 48" wide, 23" deep, 28" high, 21" drop leaves, Early Century.

BED

This term formerly referred to a feather mattress that was placed on a frame called a bedstead. See bedstead.

BEDROOM SET (or Bedchamber Suit(e))

Prior to the middle of the 1800's, furniture could be selected per piece, not as a matched set, to furnish a bedchamber. After that time one could buy either a "dressing case suit(e)" with a tall mirror and low drawers beneath, or a "bureau suit(e)," which would now be called a dresser or a chest of drawers. The dressing case was more expensive and elaborate than the bureau. Both had matching beds. Choices of coordinating washstands included the commode type with its various combination of drawers and doors; the somnoe, now known as a half commode, usually with one drawer and door; or the bureau type, a small chest of drawers. A choice of handles and mirrors, the latter often referred to as toilets or plates, could be selected by the customer.

Walnut two-piece Renaissance Revival bedroom set with burl veneer panels and applied decorations. Top photo: Bedstead, 59" wide, 102" high headboard, 49" high footboard. Bottom photo: Dressing case with marble tops in well and over handkerchief boxes, 55" wide, 21" deep, 102" high, Middle to Late Century.

Walnut two-piece Renaissance Revival bedroom set with applied burl veneer panels, applied decorations and Jelliff influenced Columbia head at pediment. Top photo: Bedstead, 62" wide, 88" high. Bottom photo: Étagère dressing case with marble tops in well and over side drawers, 55" wide, 22" deep, 93" high, Middle to Late Century.

Walnut two-piece Renaissance Revival bedroom set with burl veneer panels and applied decorations. Top photo: Bedstead, 62" wide, 92" high. Bottom photo: Dressing case with marble tops in well and over side drawers, 45" wide, 19" deep, 95" high, Middle to Late Century.

Walnut three-piece Renaissance Revival bedroom set with burl panels and applied decorations. Top left photo: Bedstead, 57" wide, 93" high headboard, 36" high footboard. Top right photo: Dressing case with marble tops in well and over side drawers, 50" wide, 19" deep, 93" high. Bottom right photo: Marble top commode washstand, 30" wide, 20" deep, 32" to marble top, 8" splash back, Middle to Late Century.

Walnut four-piece Renaissance Revival bedroom set made by Beal and Hooper, Boston, with applied decorations. Top left photo: Bedstead, 63" wide, 76" high. Bottom left photo: Marble top dresser, 42" wide, 19" deep, 87" high. Top right photo: Marble top (not original) commode washstand on legs, 32" wide, 16" deep, 38" high. Bottom right photo: Somnoe or half commode with wooden top (not original), 18" wide, 15" deep, 30" high. Middle to Late Century.

Walnut two-piece bedroom set with applied decorations. Top photo: Marble top dresser with projection front, decks and secret or slipper drawer at base, 45" wide, 22" deep, 96" high. Bottom photo: Marble top, projection front commode washstand, 33" wide, 19" deep, 31" high, 13" marble splash back, Middle Century.

Walnut two-piece bedroom set with applied burl veneer panels on drawers and mirror frame. Top photo: Marble top dresser, 40" wide, 20" deep, 82" high. Bottom photo: Marble top commode washstand, 30" wide, 16" deep, 30" high, 12" marble splash back, Late Century.

Walnut three-piece Eastlake bedroom set with incised lines and fretwork. Left photo: Dresser, 43" wide, 20" deep, 76" high. Top right photo: Commode washstand with towel bar ends, 33" wide, 19" deep, 32" high, 8" splash back. Bottom right photo: Bedstead, single size, 44" wide, 70" high headboard, 36" high footboard, Late Century.

Walnut three-piece Renaissance Revival bedroom set with burl panels and applied decorations. Top photo: Bedstead, single size, 48" wide, 99" high headboard, 35" high footboard. Marble top somnoe or half commode, 19" wide, 17" deep, 31" high. Bottom photo: Marble top dresser, 47" wide, 19" deep, 99" high, Middle to Late Century.

Walnut two-piece Eastlake bedroom set with incised lines, applied burl veneer panels and carving. Top photo: Bedstead, 59" wide, 84" high headboard, 34" high footboard. Bottom photo: Marble top dresser, 50" wide, 23" deep, 86" high, Late Century.

Flamed mahogany four-piece bedroom set made by Dauler, Close and Johns, Pittsburg, with book matched and end-to-end matched veneer on drawer fronts and panels. Top photo: Bedstead, 64" wide, 51" high headboard, 39" high footboard. Bottom left photo: Dresser, 57" wide, 25" deep, 71" high. Bottom right photo: Chiffonier or chest of drawers, 41" wide, 23" deep, 72" high. Dressing table not pictured. Late Century.

BEDSTEAD

This term, used as late as the mid-1800's, designated the frame that supported a feather bed or mattress. Today, a bed is a piece of furniture on which one sleeps.

Four poster rope bed with mahogany veneer headboard and cherry posts, 56" wide, 77" high, Middle Century.

Mahogany half-tester bedstead with mahogany veneer panels on headboard, footboard and crest, applied decorations and carving at crest, queen size, 70" wide, 114" high, 40" high footboad, Middle Century.

Walnut Eastlake half-tester bedstead with incised lines, applied burl veneer panels and decorations, single size, 43½" wide, 80" high, 10" crest, Late Century.

Walnut bedstead headboard with burl veneer panel, ring molding and applied decorations, 57" wide, 79" high headboard, 34" high footboard, Middle Century.

17

Walnut bedstead with applied decorations, 46" wide, 72" high headboard, 28" high footboard, Middle Century.

Walnut bedstead with striped walnut veneer on panels and applied decorations, 63" wide, 79" high headboard, 42" high footboard, Middle Century.

Bedstead headboard, rosewood panels and artificially grained rosewood frame, applied decorations, 65" wide, 86" high, Middle Century.

Cherry rope bedstead with blanket rail, 52" wide, 52" high, Middle Century.

BELTER, JOHN HENRY

This skillful craftsman was a trained cabinetmaker when he immigrated to the United States from Germany. He had his own shop in New York City by 1844 and died in 1863. While Belter liked rosewood, he also worked with walnut, oak and blackwood (hardwood painted to resemble ebony). His designs could be ornate or simple. Most people remember his elaborate examples with carved flowers, leaves and grapes. His realistic roses range from buds to versions in full bloom. He liked the curving rococo revival Louis XV style, and although his creations look delicate and dainty, they are actually very sturdy.

Belter patented features of his furniture craftsmanship, including a process for laminating wood credited to the ancient Egyptians. Solid wood can split when pierced, carved and bent extensively, but laminated wood withstands this torture. Because of this, John Belter glued layers of wood together so the grains of successive pieces were at right angles to each other. For example, on one layer the grain ran vertically and on the next horizontally until the desired thickness, generally from six to eight thin layers, was achieved. The number could be half or twice that according to the work to be done. Belter used steam and a special matrix (mold) to curve the wood into the desired shape. Belter frequently used intertwined leaves and flowers as connecting sweeps between pierced-carved motifs while his peers generally had C-shaped scrolls as linking mechanisms. Cabriole legs that bulge at the knee, sweep in to the ankle, then out slightly to form a double curve were favored. The front of the rear legs may be rounded but generally they were flat at the back. Casters, preferably brass, were usually placed on all four legs of chairs, not just on the front two, a procedure his competitors followed frequently.

Pierced carving was not always present, and Belter chair backs did not have to be molded into spherical, cylindrical or conical shapes that appeared to be one piece of wood when actually some of his veneer was carefully seam matched. This versatile craftsman did not always select laminated woods. He carved solid wood and at times applied the result as a crest to a frame. While parlor sets were a specialty, John Belter also made some bedroom and dining room furniture. Although most of his work is unmarked, some paper labels do exist.

Rosewood Belter, Henry Clay side chair with laminated back and carved crest, 36" high, Middle Century.

Rosewood Belter, Rosalie side chair with laminated back and carved roses and grapes on crest, 37" high, Middle Century.

BOOKCASE

A bookcase is a frame with shelves where books are stored.

Walnut Eastlake single door bookcase with incised lines and carving, 29" wide, 14" deep, 64" high, 8" pediment, Late Century.

Walnut Eastlake single door bookcase with spoon carving and incised lines, 31" wide, 13" deep, 59" high, Late Century.

BUFFET (or Sideboard)

A buffet is a dining room piece with drawers and cupboards used to hold items such as china, silver and linens.

Walnut double door bookcase with applied burl veneer panels and decorations, 52" wide, 15" deep, 65" high, Late Century.

Walnut Renaissance Revival marble top buffet with applied burl veneer panels and decorations, 57" wide, 23" deep, 84" high, Middle to Late Century.

BUREAU (or a Chest of Drawers or Dresser)

A bureau is a chest of drawers or a dresser where clothes are kept. It could be purchased with or without a toilet or plate, two obsolete terms for a mirrror.

Walnut bureau washstand with incised lines, 31" wide, 18" deep, 29" high, 7" backsplash, Late Century.

BUTLER'S DESK

Customarily a butler stood up to do his necessary household book work at a desk with a leaf that resembled a drawer but dropped down to form a writing surface. Beneath it were more drawers, enough to form a tall desk.

Walnut marble top bureau or dresser with burl panels, applied decorations and a secret or slipper drawer at base, 47" wide, 23" deep, 85" high, Middle Century.

BUREAU WASHSTAND

Customarily this was a small chest of drawers with either two parallel drawers above two full length ones or with three full length drawers. Some had towel bar extensions at each end. At times a retractable (pushes in and pulls out when needed) towel bar was available. Personal cleansing articles, including a washbowl and pitcher, were kept in or on it.

Cherry butler's desk with imitation top drawer that drops to form writing surface and reveals desk compartments with maple veneer drawer fronts, 45" wide, 23" deep, 45" high, Middle Century.

C

CABINET (or Cupboard)

A storage case, usually with shelves or drawers, used to hold items, is exemplified by a china cabinet.

Mahogany curio cabinet with fretwork and cabriole legs, 28" wide, 14" deep, 60" high, Late Century.

Top right photo: Walnut Eastlake dental cabinet with incised lines, spoon carving and side drawers, 32" wide, 19" deep, 65" high, Late Century.

Bottom right photo: Walnut marble top barber's cabinet with incised lines and applied burl veneer panels, 29" wide, 19" deep, 35" high, Late Century.

Walnut dental cabinet with applied burl veneer panels, decorations, burl drawer fronts and marble surfaces, 34" wide, 21" deep, 73" high, Middle Century.

CANDLESTAND

A small table that originally held a candlestick is referred to as a candlestand.

Walnut marble top candlestand with applied decorations, 15" diameter, 31" high, Middle Century.

CANOPY BED (or Tester Bed)

When a framework similar to a roof is supported by posts on a bed, it is called a canopy or a tester bed. If this frame extends only over the head portion and not the entire length, it is referred to as a half-tester.

Mahogany and mahogany veneered canopy or full-tester Empire transitional bedstead with applied decorations, 69" wide, 95" high, Early Century.

CANTERBURY

Originally a canterbury was a portable stand with dividers and was developed in the 1800's to hold sheet music. Today this piece is considered a magazine rack.

Walnut canterbury or magazine rack with base drawer, 23" wide, 14" deep, 17" high, Late Century.

Walnut canterbury or magazine rack with molded frame and applied decorations, 24" wide, 16" deep, 35" high, Late Century.

CARD TABLE (or Game Table)

A table that generally folds in some manner and is used for playing cards or other games is a card or game table. During the 1800's many had double tops and could assume two additional positions. The folded portion could be opened out to double the size when in use, or one half might lie flat on its legs or pedestal while the other half could stand up against the wall. Some types included a hidden drawer where games or cards were kept. Other versions do not fold.

Mahogany Empire pedestal game table that can assume three positions, has paw feet, 36" wide, 18" deep, 30" high, Early Century.

CENTRE TABLE

A rather large, usually decorative table that was placed in the middle of a Victorian parlor is referred to as a centre table. An 1876 price list spells "center" with an "re" instead or "er".

Walnut marble top center table with bun feet, 35" wide, 26" deep, 28" high, Late century.

CHAIR

A chair is a piece of furniture that commonly consists of four legs, a back and a seat on which one person can sit. There are many types. For example: an arm chair, as the name implies, has arm rests for the comfort of the sitter. A Belter chair is one made by the craftsman, John Belter. A cane example has a woven rattan seat. The back may be woven also. A gentleman's chair is a large upholstered arm chair where a man could sit comfortably. A lady's chair might match it but was daintier. A woman's floor length skirt with its yards and yards of material could be better accommodated in a chair without arms. Photographers liked to have their clients pose seated in or standing beside fancy chairs. These chairs became known as photographer's chairs.

Mahogany Chippendale arm chair, 22" arm to arm, 36" high, Early Century or late 1700's.

Rosewood upholstered arm chair with tufted back, open arms and cabriole legs, 24" arm to arm, 40" high, Middle Century.

Rosewood upholstered arm chair with open arms and cabriole legs, 26" arm to arm, 39" high, Middle Century.

Walnut upholstered arm chair with tufted back, applied decorations, dolphin arm supports and dolphins on crest, 23" arm to arm, 44" high, Middle Century.

Jelliff influenced walnut upholstered arm chair with tufted back, open arms and carved head on crest, 28" arm to arm, 42" high, Middle to Late Century.

Walnut Eastlake upholstered arm chair with open arms and incised lines, 27" arm to arm, 39" high, Late Century.

Walnut Eastlake upholstered arm chair with tufted back, open arms, incised lines and carving, 28" arm to arm, 38" high, Late Century.

Walnut cane-seat arm chair with burl decorations and open arms, 21" arm to arm, 39" high, Late Century.

Walnut Eastlake transitional cane-seat and cane-back arm chair with incised lines and open arms, 22" arm to arm, 40" high, Late Century.

Walnut pressed cane kitchen chair with lyre splat and burl panel on crest, 38" high, Late Century.

Rosewood Belter, Rosalie side chair with laminated back and carved roses and grapes on crest, 37" high, Middle Century.

Walnut cane-seat chair with flat front rung, 34" high, Middle Century.

Walnut cane-seat chair with burl decorations on crest, 34" high, Middle Century.

Walnut cane-seat chair with burl veneer decorations on slats and crest rail, 34" high, Late Century.

Walnut cane-seat chair with balloon back, 34" high, Middle Century.

Walnut Eastlake transitional cane-seat, cane-back chair with incised lines and burl veneer decorations, 34" high, Late Century.

Walnut cane-seat chair with burl decorations on splat and crest, 35" high, Middle Century.

Rosewood upholstered gentleman's chair with open arms and tufted back, 23" arm to arm, 40" high, Middle Century.

Walnut Eastlake cane-seat, cane-back swivel, tilt back office chair with incised lines and burl veneer decorations, 23" arm to arm, 39" high, Late Century.

Rosewood upholstered gentleman's chair with open arms, tufted back and carved crest, 25" arm to arm, 43" high, Middle Century.

Walnut lady's chair, Louis XV substyle, with tufted back, finger roll and rose carving on crest and apron, 26" arm to arm, 39" high, Middle Century.

Walnut Renaissance Revival lady's chair with tufted back, burl veneer and applied decorations, 38" high, Middle Century.

Walnut Eastlake transitional lady's chair with Minerva head on crest, incised lines, applied burl veneer panels and decorations, 36" high, Middle Century.

Walnut Louis XV substyle lady's chair with continuous frame to apron, finger roll and cabriole legs, 38" high, Middle Century.

Walnut Louis XV substyle lady's and gentleman's matching chairs with original horsehair upholstery, button back, finger roll and cabriole legs. Lady's chair: 23" wide, 41" high; Gentleman's chair: 25" arm to arm, 43" high. Middle Century.

Walnut Louis XV substyle lady's and gentleman's matching chairs with tufted backs, continuous finger roll frame to apron and cabriole legs. Lady's chair: 40" high; Gentleman's chair: 25" arm to arm, 45" high. Middle Century.

Walnut Louis XV substyle lady's and gentleman's matching chairs with finger roll oval back and cabriole legs. Lady's chair: 23" between hip rests, 39" high; Gentleman's chair: 27" arm to arm, 42" high. Middle Century.

Walnut Louis XV substyle lady's and gentleman's matching chairs with finger roll oval back and cabriole legs. Lady's chair: 22" between hip rests, 38" high; Gentleman's chair: 25" arm to arm, 40" high. Middle Century.

Right photo: Rosewood photographer's chair with carving on crest, lower back and apron, 39" high, Middle to Late Century.

Walnut and walnut burl Empire side chair with splat back and slip seat, 33" high, Early Century.

Mahogany veneered side chair with applied carved crest and slip seat, 34" high, Middle Century.

Mahogany veneered Empire side chair with splat back and slip seat, 33" high, Early Century.

Walnut Empire side chair with carved crest and slat, slip seat and original horsehair upholstery, 33" high, Early Century.

Mahogany Empire side chair with lyre splat, 31" high, Early Century.

Walnut Louis XV substyle rococo side chair with fruit C-scroll, fruit and nut carving, tufted back and ebonized decorations, 2⊆" arm to arm, 42" high, Middle Century.

Walnut side chair with tufted back, interlocking C-scroll and carved roses on crest, 39" high, Middle Century.

Walnut Louis XV substyle rococo side chair with tufted back, morning glory, grapes and leaves carved on crest and cabriole legs, 38" high, Middle Century.

Rosewood Louis XV substyle side chair with tufted back, open work on back, carved crest and cabriole legs, 38" high, Middle Century.

Walnut side chair with carved roses on crest and cabriole legs, 36" high, Middle Century.

Rosewood Louis XV substyle rococo side chair with carved splat and crest and cabriole legs, 36" high, Middle Century.

Rosewood rococo side chair with upholstered leaf panel on back and carved leaves and grapes, 43" high, Middle Century.

Walnut Louis XV substyle side chair with a carved and pierced crest, 35" high, Middle Century.

Walnut side chair (originally caned) with a balloon back, 37" high, Middle Century.

Walnut Louis XV substyle balloon back side chair with burl decorations on crest, 36" high, Middle Century.

Walnut Renaissance Revival side chair with Eastlake influence and burl veneer panels and applied decorations, 39" high, Middle to Late Century.

Walnut Eastlake side chair with incised lines and burl decorations, 38" high, Late Century.

Walnut Eastlake side chair with tufted back and incised lines, 36" high, Late Century.

CHEST OF DRAWERS (or Chiffonier or Sidelock)

An upright piece of furniture containing a series of drawers in a frame. See Chiffonier, Dresser, and Sidelock.

Walnut Renaissance Revival side chair with Eastlake influence, tufted back, incised lines, burl and applied decorations, 36" high, Middle to Late Century.

Cherry projection front sidelock chest with incised lines and burl veneer drawer fronts, 29" wide, 19" deep, 45" high, Late Century.

CHIFFONIER (or Chest of Drawers or Sidelock)

An 1876 catalogue spelling for a tall, narrow chest of drawers was "cheffonier." Some are called sidelocks because the hinged stile closes to lock all the drawers simultaneously.

Walnut chiffonier or chest of drawers with molded burl panels on drawers and applied decorations, 39" wide, 19" deep, 66" high, Late Century.

CHINA CABINET

A china cabinet or closet has glass panels so that it serves as a show case for porcelain, china, glass and similar articles.

Mahogany china cabinet with roll and scroll stiles and a convex glass door, 50" wide, 22" deep, 62" high, Late Century.

COMMODE WASHSTAND
(or Somnoe or Half Commode)

A washstand that combines a drawer or drawers with a cupboard space is called a commode washstand. A small version that commonly has only one drawer and door is known as a somnoe or half commode.

Walnut commode washstand with molded burl panels on drawer and doors, 30" wide, 18" deep, 30" high, 8" splash back, Late Century.

COMMON WASHSTAND

This term describes a table, usually with towel bar ends, on which a wash bowl and pitcher were placed in the days before inside plumbing. A lower shelf was also included.

Walnut common washstand with towel bar ends, 25" arm to arm, 15" deep, 29" high, 4" splash back, Late Century.

CORNER CUPBOARD

A triangular cabinet shaped to hang or stand in a corner is called a corner cupboard.

Cherry corner cupboard, one piece, 56" wide, 28" deep, 85" high, Early Century or late 1700's.

Cherry corner cupboard, one piece, 46" wide, 20" deep, 90" high, Middle Century.

Cherry corner cupboard, one piece, 48" wide, 19" deep, 85" high, Middle Century.

Cherry corner cupboard, one piece, 34" wide, 21" deep, 76" high, Middle Century.

Walnut cradle that swings on frame, 42" wide, 20" deep, 35" high, Middle Century.

Walnut corner cupboard, one piece, with one drawer, 44" wide, 18" deep, 80" high, Middle Century.

CUPBOARD (or Cabinet)

A cupboard is an enclosed case with shelves for holding food, cups, plates, linens and other objects.

CRADLE

This refers to a baby's small bed that rocks on rockers or sways suspended from a frame.

Walnut cradle on rockers, 38" wide, 20" deep, 23" high, Middle Century.

Cherry and walnut two-piece closed cupboard, 50" wide, 21" deep at base, 81" high, Early Century.

Walnut two-piece closed cupboard, 40" wide, 20" deep at base, 74" high, Middle Century.

Cherry two-piece step-back cupboard, 47" wide, 21" deep at base, 84" high, Middle Century.

Cherry and mahogany two-piece step-back cupboard, 48" wide, 19" deep at base, 81" high, Middle Century.

Walnut two-piece step-back cupboard, 42" wide, 20" deep at base, 84" high, Middle Century.

Walnut cupboard with closed bottom and open top for display purposes, 63" wide, 18" deep, 74" high, early 20th century.

CYLINDER DESK (or Secretary)

A cylinder desk or secretary has a quarter round, rolling, solid not slatted section that pushes up and back to make a writing area available to the user. It pulls down again to cover the writing surface when it is not in use. The secretary type includes a bookcase section also.

Walnut cylinder front secretary with burl veneer on cylinder and drawer front, 33" wide, 23" deep, 82" high, Middle to Late Century.

✎∽ **D** ∽✎

DAVENPORT DESK

This small desk, popular in the mid-1800's, usually had a sloping lift lid writing surface over a storage space and drawers that pull out at the side instead of at the front.

Walnut day bed or window seat, 75" wide, 27" deep, Late Century.

Walnut lift top davenport desk with burl veneer panels and door on the side (vertical dividers inside), 27" wide, 22" deep, 52" high, Middle Century.

DESK

A desk provides its user with a flat or sloping surface for writing, reading or drawing and with drawers, compartments or cupboards for storing pens, pencils, papers, books or related objects.

DAY BED

A daybed is usually narrow with low head and foot boards of equal height. It can serve as a couch by day. Some have a pull-out section that nearly doubles the sleeping area. At times it is referred to as a hired man's bed because the extra help employed on a farm often slept on such a bed.

Mahogany and rosewood butler's desk with drop front writing surface that resembles a drawer when closed, 43" wide, 20" deep, 44" high, Middle Century.

Walnut day bed or window seat with blanket roll ends, 57" wide, 26" deep, Late Century.

Mahogany Empire butler's secretary with writing surface that resembles a drawer when closed, 42" wide, 22" deep, 82" high, Middle Century.

Walnut cylinder front secretary with applied burl veneer panels and decorations, 35" wide, 22" deep, 95" high, Middle Century.

Walnut cylinder front desk with burl decorations and a carved pediment, 30" wide, 24" deep, 61" high, Middle Century.

Walnut cylinder front secretary with applied burl veneer panels, 40" wide, 23" deep, 92" high, Middle Century.

Walnut Eastlake cylinder front secretary with applied burl decorations, 37" wide, 22" deep, 84" high, Late Century.

Walnut Eastlake drop front parlor desk with incised lines and burl panels, 26" wide, 56" deep, Late Century.

Walnut Eastlake drop front parlor desk with marble top and burl panels on drawer fronts, 34" wide, 18" deep, 53" high, Late Century.

Walnut Eastlake lift top davenport desk with incised lines, burl panels and three drawers on the side, 30" wide, 22" deep, 43" high, Late Century.

Walnut Eastlake drop front secretary with incised lines, burl veneer panels and applied decorations, 30" wide, 17" deep, 86" high, Late Century.

Walnut Renaissance Revival bookcase secretary with fold-out writing surface, applied decorations and ring molding, 48" wide, 21" deep, 95" high, Middle Century.

Walnut knee hole desk, 53" wide, 32" deep, 31" high, 5" back rail, Late Century.

695

Walnut drop front table desk with storage section under lift lid at top, 38" wide, 21" deep, 58" high, Middle Century.

2890

Mahogany veneer, cherry and pine Empire secretary with fold-out writing surface, 41" wide, 20" deep, 77" high, Early Century.

2000

Walnut slant front secretary with incised lines, burl veneer panels and applied decorations, 39" wide, 21" deep, 89" high, Late Century.

2500

Rosewood and walnut slant front desk with applied decorations, 37" wide, 18" deep, 71" high, Middle Century.

Rosewood slant front desk with applied and carved decorations, molded panels and back rail, 38" deep, 20" wide, 49" high, Middle Century. Right photo: View of desk interior.

Mahogany Empire whatnot desk with tiger maple drawer fronts in writing section, 38" wide, 20" deep, 60" high, Early Century.

Walnut slant front secretary with burl veneer panels, 39" wide, 20" deep, 84" high, Middle Century.

DINING ROOM SUIT(E) (or Dining Room Set)

A dining room set can include a table with chairs that match in style and in the wood used. Large sets might also have a buffet or sideboard, a china cabinet, a server, and a tea cart.

Mahogany eleven-piece dining room set made by Berkey and Gay, Grand Rapids, Michigan, that includes one arm chair, 22" arm to arm, 30" high; seven side chairs, 37" high; round dining room table with pedestal base, 60" diameter, 30" high; buffet, 72" wide, 23" deep, 39" high; china cabinet with two doors and convex sides, 50" wide, 19" deep, 61" high. Late Century.

DRESSER (or Bureau or Chest of Drawers)

A dresser is a chest of drawers for storing clothing. It usually has a mirror.

Bottom right photo: Mahogany chest on frame made by Samuel Prince, 1760-1790, 44" wide, 24" deep, 56" high, late 18th Century.

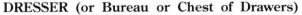

Cherry, mahogany veneer and maple veneer Empire dresser with scroll feet, 40" wide, 20" deep, 41" high, 5" high decks, Early Century.

Cherry Empire dresser, 43" wide, 21" deep, 45" high, Early Century.

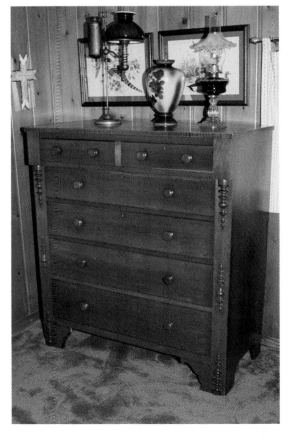

Mahogany crotch veneer Empire dresser with scalloped apron, decks and back rail, 37" wide, 18" deep, 34" high, Early Century.

Cherry Empire projection front dresser with applied decorations and tiger maple stiles and top, 44" wide, 21" deep, 49" high, Early Century.

Cherry dresser with decks and applied decorations, 40" wide, 18" deep, 36" high, 5" deck, Middle Century.

Walnut projection front dresser with original mirror and decks missing, 43" wide, 19" deep, 42" high, Middle Century.

Walnut étagère rococo marble top dresser with boxes and applied decorations. Drawers framed with applied molding. 53" wide, 25" deep, 87" high, Middle Century.

Walnut Renaissance Revival marble top dresser with molded burl veneer panels and applied decorations, 30" wide, 18" deep, 91" high, Middle Century.

Walnut marble top dresser with molded burl veneer panels, applied decorations, swing mirror and boxes, 44" wide, 21" deep, 94" high, Middle Century.

Walnut marble top dresser with feather veneered drawer fronts, applied circular molding, center grape carved handles and swing mirror attached to box, 43" wide, 20" deep, 80" high, Middle Century.

Crotch mahogany Empire marble top dresser, applied decorations, serpentine front and swing mirror, 44" wide, 21" deep, 80" high, Early Century.

Walnut marble top dresser with matched mahogany veneer on drawer fronts applied decorations, swing mirror and decks, 42" wide, 20' deep, 79" high, Middle Century.

Walnut marble insert dresser with burl veneer drawer fronts, applied decorations, circular molding, wishbone mirror and decks, 41" wide, 20" deep, 72" high, Late Century.

Walnut marble top dresser with applied burl veneer panels, applied decorations, swing mirror and boxes, 42" wide, 18" deep, 77" high, Late Century.

Walnut marble top dresser with applied burl veneer panels, circular and ring molding, swing mirror, boxes and secret drawer at base, 42" wide, 20" deep, 84" high, Late Century.

Walnut marble top dresser with applied decorations, ring molding, fretwork on mirror frame, swing mirror, boxes and secret drawer at base, 42" wide, 21" deep, 87" high, Late Century.

Walnut Renaissance Revival marble top cheval mirror dresser with burl veneer drawer fronts and three secret drawers at base with applied circular molding decorations, 55" wide, 18" deep, 72" high, Middle to Late Century.

Walnut and rosewood wig dresser with marble insert, burl veneer facing compartments within hinged vertical side doors at outside top and base, 48" wide, 21" deep, 84" high, Middle Century.

Rosewood marble top rococo dresser with applied decorations and serpentine front, 43" wide, 21" deep, 44" high, Middle Century.

Bottom right photo: Artificially grained rosewood marble top wig dresser with compartments within hinged doors on each side of swing mirror, 42" wide, 20" deep, 71" high, Middle Century.

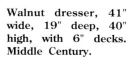

Walnut dresser, 41" wide, 19" deep, 40" high, with 6" decks. Middle Century.

Cherry dresser with mahogany book matched veneer on drawer fronts and wishbone mirror, 41" wide, 19" deep, 71" high, 6" deck, Middle Century.

DRESSING CASE

A dressing case is often called a step down or well dresser. The well is flanked by small drawers that form the sides of the well. Beneath are frequently two full length drawers. The surface of the well and the tops of the small drawers are often covered with marble. (See Bedroom Set.)

DRESSING TABLE

This table had a mirror called plate or toilet in the 1800's. A person could sit in front of it to complete his or her toilet (comb hair, arrange clothing, etc.).

Walnut projection front dresser with mahogany veneered drawer fronts, applied decorations and ring molding, 41" wide, 19" deep, 32" high, 6" deck, Middle Century.

Mahogany dressing table with carved legs, mirror surround and stretchers, Middle Century. Covered glass dome on table top shows a wicker basket filled with wax fruit.

DRY SINK

Usually a dry sink was a kitchen utility piece. It had an open tray top and was generally zinc lined with a cupboard beneath. Some people suggest that the slurring of the word "zinc" resulted in the term assigned to the piece – "sink."

Walnut dry sink with display shelves, 58" wide, 19" deep, 64" high, Late Century.

EASEL

An easel is a tripod or upright frame used to display a picture.

Left photo: Walnut easel with carved leaf and grape finial, 19" wide, 78" high, Late Century.

Right photo: Walnut carved easel, 21" wide, 71" high, Late Century.

EASTLAKE, CHARLES LOCK(E) - England

Charles Eastlake rebelled against overly ornate furniture, curved lines, and inferior furniture turned out cheaply and rapidly by machines without any thought being given to its design. In 1868, he expressed his views in his book, *Hints on Household Taste*. He felt simple, straight lines did not waste wood and were attractive and stronger than curved ornate furniture. He wanted furniture to be designed well and machines to be used wisely to produce quality products. Eastlake liked to work with oak wood and enjoyed using Gothic and Japanese designs. From the 1870's through the 1890's, United States factories followed his ideas but they used walnut and cherry (the latter sometimes a cherry stain) and added appendages, moldings, incised lines, and chip carving to his boxy, rectangular lines.

When parallel cut-in lines appear on such Eastlake pieces, today's antiquers refer to them as railroad tracks. Eastlake helped to modernize styles and to introduce conscious design to the furniture industry.

Walnut Eastlake drop front parlor desk with incised lines, burl veneer drawer fronts and applied panels, 26" wide, 15" deep, 56" high, Late Century.

EMPIRE

The Empire style of furniture was produced in the United States from circa 1815-1840. It was named for France's Emperor Napoleon Bonaparte. The French versions were very extravagant and massive, incorporating details borrowed from ancient Greek, Roman, and Egyptian designs. Mahogany, rosewood, and ebony were the rich woods used and brass and gilt mounts abounded. The latter were incorporated in torches, wreaths, swags, and laurel branches. Emblems that honored the ruler included the crown, the letter "N", and a bee. These were on the furniture as well as in the fabrics. Egyptian figures, including the sphinx, as well as other mythological creatures, were used. While American Empire furniture tended to be massive, it generally was not as ornately decorated as the French versions. Although rosewood and ebony were used, mahogany was the leader, so much so that, in the United States, this period is called the "Age of Mahogany." Features included thick lyre bases, pillars and scrolls, beading, wings as feet on sofas, rectangular shapes, acanthus leaf and laurel branch swags, ogee (a molding with a double continuous curve) frames, and claw feet. A symmetrical look was achieved by using a column on one side on a furniture stile balanced by a similar column on the opposite side. Round wooden pulls or lion head back plates with ring pulls were popular handles. Both marble tops and wooden ones were used. The early Empire furniture was made by hand by craftsmen, but the factory system with its newly invented steam-operated band saw changed the industry. When rows of bedsteads, tables, chests and chairs could be produced rapidly by machines, the cabinetmaker with his personal relationship to his customers began to disappear. Of course, some furniture makers did continue to embellish their works with hand-carved extras.

Walnut full-length mirror étagère with marble top over serpentine drawer, applied decorations and carved and fretwork pediment, 56" wide, 17" deep, 94" high, Middle Century.

Mahogany Empire dresser with book matched veneer drawer fronts, ogee top drawer and scroll feet, 44" wide, 21" deep, 48" high, Early Century.

ÉTAGÈRE (or Whatnot)

A large and fancy whatnot is generally called an etagere. Mirrors in back of shelves may be present to help display the fine collectibles or bric-a-brac to better advantage. Sometimes marble is present. Most versions sat flat against the wall, but there are corner ones also. Some had an enclosed cupboard base. Occasionally fancy shelves were combined with a desk or dresser to form an étagère desk or dresser.

Artificially grained rosewood étagère with marble top over drawer and carved and fretwork pediment, 54" wide, 19" deep, 89" high, Middle Century.

Walnut full-length mirror étagère with marble top over drawer at base, cabriole legs and fretwork back, 50" wide, 21" deep, 93" high, Middle Century. Covered glass dome on marble displays a selection of stuffed birds.

Walnut étagère with half mirror, applied decorations, open molded panels and a drawer at the base, 52" wide, 16" deep, 81" high, Middle Century.

Rosewood étagère with a drawer at the base and fretwork under shelves and at pediment, 41" wide, 16" deep, 64" high, Middle Century.

Walnut étagère with half mirror and drawer under second shelf from the top and molded mirror surrounds and back supports, 44" wide, 15" deep, 77" high, Middle Century.

Artificially grained rosewood over walnut marble top ètagére with ornate carvings, 48" wide, 18" deep, 86" high, Middle Century.

Walnut ètagére with rosewood graining, drawer under marble top, applied decorations and fretwork pediment, 43" wide, 18" deep, 80" high, Middle Century.

Rosewood marble top ètagére with fretwork at pediment, applied decorations and a base that contains 3 drawers, side shelves and a door with an insert mirror, 50" side, 19" deep, 99" high, Middle Century.

Rosewood marble top ètagére with applied decorations and carving, a single bow front drawer over a circular door at center base that spins around to open, 69" wide, 27" deep, 86" high, Middle Century.

FIREPLACE MANTEL

A mantel is a structure around and above a fireplace. In England it is called a fireplace surround.

Walnut fireplace mantel with burl veneer facing, 60" wide, 13" deep, 48" high, Late Century.

Walnut ètagére with burl veneer facing, applied decorations, a fretwork pediment and a mirrored door at base outlined with fretwork, 37" wide, 18" deep, 68" high, Late Century.

FIRE SCREEN

This is an adjustable panel on a pole used as a shield to protect a person from the direct heat of a fireplace. Usually they are small and moveable. Wooden, needlework, and papier maché versions are available.

Walnut corner ètagére with two marble shelves and a mirrored back and applied decorations, 27" wide, 18" deep, 76" high, Middle Century.

Mahogany fireplace screen with leaf carving and a needlepoint center design, 26" wide, 58" high, Middle Century.

FIRESIDE FOLDING ROCKER

This rocking chair could be placed by the fireplace and could be folded up when not in use. Customarily, its wooden frame had an upholstered back and seat.

Walnut footstool with cabriole legs and molded apron, 20" wide, 15" deep, 15" high, Middle Century.

Walnut folding fireside rocker with upholstered back and seat and burl veneer panels, 34" high, Late Century.

Walnut footstool with molded apron and legs, 22" wide, 14" deep, 17" high, Late Century.

FOOTSTOOL

This is a low stool upon which a seated person's feet can be supported.

Mahogany Empire footstool with scroll feet, 22" wide, 16" deep, 17" high, Early Century.

Walnut double roll footstool with applied roundels, 19" wide, 11" deep, 10' high, Late Century.

GAME TABLE (or Card Table)

Tables on which games are played are designed in the style of the period in which they were made. Many fold in some manner. Some tops can swivel. One form with a hinged top can assume three positions. It can be folded down to have a double top or half can be supported by the wall while one half covers the base. When both pieces are parallel, a wide playing surface is achieved. There may be an enclosed space where games are kept.

Walnut game table that can assume three positions has a blue felt insert with carved and applied decorations on base and apron, 36" wide, 18" deep, 30" high, Middle Century.

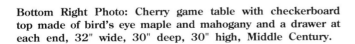

Walnut game table that can assume three positions has burl veneer on ogee apron, 36" wide, 18" deep, 30" high, Middle Century.

Bottom Right Photo: Cherry game table with checkerboard top made of bird's eye maple and mahogany and a drawer at each end, 32" wide, 30" deep, 30" high, Middle Century.

GOTHIC

Gothic furniture was not produced in abundance. Some was made from the 1820's to the 1850's and there was a brief revival of the style in the 1870's. It has a cathedral-like feel. Pointed arches, delicate tracery (lattice-like lines that resemble the framework on ornate church windows), and steeple shapes on clocks and chair backs are present. Most gothic furniture has a light, almost delicate appearance.

GRANDFATHER CHAIR

An oversized, upholstered gentleman's chair with arms.

Mahogany gothic child's chair with needlepoint seat, 33" high, Middle Century. Standing beside chair is a German Simon-Halbig bisque doll.

Mahogany Louis XV substyle grandfather's chair with tufted back, rose and leaf carved crest, finger roll and cabriole legs, 28" arm to arm, 46" high, Middle Century.

H

HALF COMMODE (or Somnoe)

A half commode is a small washstand, usually with one drawer and one door. Today many people call it a half commode because of its size.

HALL TREE (or Stand)

As its name implies, this piece of furniture was placed in the entry way of homes as a receptacle for hats, coats, umbrellas, etc. A mirror, coat hooks, and metal drip pans for the wet umbrellas were features.

Walnut marble top half commode with burl veneer facing and applied decorations, 19" wide, 20" deep, 33" high, Middle Century.

HALF-TESTER BED

When a roof-like covering suspended on two high posts flanking the headboard extends over the head portion only of a bed, this canopy forms a half-tester bed. Net curtains to keep out mosquitoes were attached to the frames Prudent Mallard designed for his Louisiana customers.

Top right photo: Mahogany half-tester bedstead with applied decorations and burl veneer on headboard and tester surround, 63" wide, 89" high, Middle Century.

Bottom right photo: Walnut hall tree or stand with fretwork on mirror surround and pediment, marble top over drawer and umbrella holders, 36" wide, 17" deep, 82" high, Middle Century.

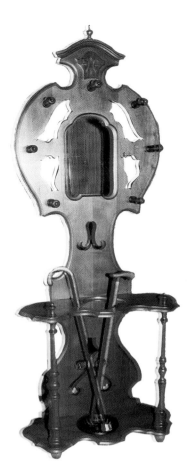

Walnut hall tree with seven turned hat holders, mirror and open hole in center for umbrellas or canes, 32" wide, 18" deep, 83" high, Late Century.

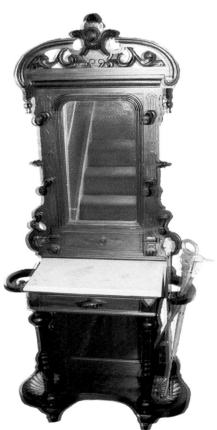

Top left photo: Walnut hall tree with eight turned hat holders, a drawer, oval mirror and full width drip pan at base, 30" wide, 18" deep, 82" high, Late Century.

Bottom left photo: Walnut Renaissance Revival hall tree with Eastlake influence, incised line, applied decorations, marble top over drawer and umbrella holders, 38" wide, 14" deep, 82" high, Middle to Late Century.

HANGING WALL CABINET (or Cupboard)

A hanging wall cabinet can be attached to a flat wall or a triangular type can occupy a corner spot.

Walnut hanging cupboard with molded frame and applied grapes and leaf decoration on door, 20" wide, 13" deep, 28" high, Late Century.

HUNZINGER, GEORGE

This furniture maker patented a folding chair in 1861 and other patents followed. He opened his shop in 1866 in New York City where his production included folding chairs and others to resemble folding types, rockers, and office chairs. The "Hunzinger" name was generally stamped on his works. "N.Y." and the patent date could be included. He died in 1898.

Walnut Hunzinger rocker with wire in seat and back that was originally cloth wrapped. The date, April 10, 1876, is impressed on leg, 21" arm to arm, 33" high, Late Century.

JELLIFF, JOHN

John Jelliff had a shop in Newark, New Jersey from 1836-1860. He made furniture with cutout gothic arches and in the rococo styles. Later he turned to Renaissance Revival with its bulkier, rectangular look and generous amounts of applied decorations and appendages. The woods Jelliff favored were rosewood and walnut. He carved solid wooden caryatids (females) with long flowing hair and warrior-like atlantes (males) as sofa and chair arm supports. Sometimes he merely used carved heads. Other designers marketed similar styles but currently works with these characteristics are attributed to Jelliff, marked "made in the Jelliff manner" or are described as resembling his work, even though they have not been documented as coming from his shop. Many collectors appreciate this man's quality craftsmanship as he was a master carver. He died in 1893.

JELLY CUPBOARD

This cupboard served as a storage unit in a Victorian kitchen or pantry. Many housewives in rural areas filled jars with jams and jellies made from berries and other fruits that they picked during the summer months. Since such cupboards were utilitarian, not ornamental pieces, their designated purpose was to hold food for the family to use during the winter.

Walnut Jelliff upholstered master or grandfather's chair, applied decorations and carved female head arm supports, 28" arm to arm, 45" high, Middle Century.

Walnut and cherry jelly cupboard with molded panels, 45" wide, 19" deep, 49" high, Late Century.

Walnut jelly cupboard, 44" wide, 16" deep, 46" high, Middle to Late Century.

K

KNEE HOLE DESK

Desks with an opening between the two banks of drawers or storage doors are so designated because they allow room to accommodate the sitter's knees.

Top right photo: Mahogany knee hole desk with marble top and applied decorations on drawers, 46" wide, 24" deep, 29" high, Middle Century.

L

LAMP TABLE

Among the various small tables in Victorian parlors were those on which lamps stood. These followed the current furniture style. For example, for Louis XV rococo, round, oval or scalloped tops appeared. Renaissance Revival featured rectanglar tops with ornate bases while Eastlake versions were rectilinear with incised lines and chip carving.

Bottom right photo: Walnut oval marble top lamp table with molded apron and base, 21" wide, 17" deep, 28" high, Late Century.

LIBRARY TABLE

Ordinarily a library table has a rather large top, a drawer, and possibly a base shelf. It provided a place where writing supplies, books, magazines, and newspapers could be kept.

LIFT TOP COMMODE

When the top of a commode washstand is hinged, it will lift up to show where a bowl and pitcher were kept for personal cleansing in pre-plumbing days. A fake drawer parallel to a real drawer was found on the side where the well dropped to a lower level to accommodate the pitcher. Some lift top commodes had towel bar ends.

Walnut Renaissance Revival library table with Eastlake influence and burl veneered top and drawer front, 36" wide, 21" deep, 30" high, Middle to Late Century.

Walnut lift top commode with two doors, 31" wide, 17" deep, 32" high, Late Century.

Walnut lift top commode with one drawer and two doors, 32" wide, 17" deep, 31" high, Late Century.

Walnut lift top commode with towel bar ends, applied burl veneer panel and two doors, 31" wide, 37" arm to arm, 18" deep, 6" splash back, Late Century.

LOUIS XV REVIVAL FURNITURE
(or Rococo Style)

Louis XV was King of France from 1643-1715. During his reign, the feminine rococo style of furniture was popular. The curved line was stressed with nature providing the inspiration for decorations that featured carved rocks, shells, fruits, flowers, leaves and nuts. The cabriole leg appeared on tables, chairs, and sofas. It is shaped to resemble a goat's leg and bulged at the knee, flowed in, and then swelled outward at the ankle. Marble tops were common. French examples were much more elaborate than their United States counterparts since gilt and brass were used generously, but Louis XV styles did influence the rococo furniture that enhanced American homes from about 1840-1865.

Walnut Louis XV Revival medallion back sofa with tufted back, finger roll and cabriole legs, 55" arm to arm, Middle Century.

M

MALLARD, PRUDENT

Prudent Mallard, a skilled New Orleans, Louisiana craftsman from about 1838 to the 1870's, seemed to enjoy making tall furniture for the high ceiling rooms in southern plantations. He carved graceful short-haired caryatids (female figures used as supporting columns). Frequently, he created floral sprays or a cabochon (an egg-like design made to resemble a gem or polished stone) for crests or for the aprons on such pieces as dressing tables. He liked serpentine drawers that wiggled in and out across the front of furniture. While rosewood was his preference, he also worked with mahogany, walnut and oak. His main creations were in the Rococo and Renaissance Revival styles. Besides his own designs, he imported furniture from England and France. Tradition states that his imported wares bore the Mallard stamp while his own works were unmarked. Large, extra tall half-tester beds on which the canopy or roof-like top covering extended out over only the head of the beds, had net curtains to keep mosquitoes away from the sleepers. Many of his large armoires (wardrobes) had secret drawers. Some experts rank Mallard with John Belter as an excellent Victorian craftsman. Quality furniture is sometimes described as having Mallard characteristics when it bears a resemblance to his known works.

MEDALLION BACK SOFA

A medallion is a large medal or an ornament or design shaped to resemble one. At times an oval, round or square area of upholstery can be framed with wood to become the focal point in the middle of the back of a sofa. The cloth inside this area can be tufted. When such a decoration is present, the sofa is referred to as a medallion back sofa.

Rosewood marble top dressing table in the Mallard manner with caryatid supports for swing mirror, applied decorations and a serpentine drawer, 42" wide, 21" deep, 66" high, Early Century.

Photo below: Walnut medallion button back sofa with grape and leaf decorated crest, 63" arm to arm, Early Century.

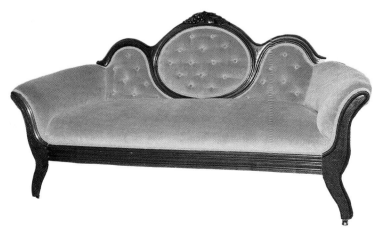

MEEKS, JOSEPH

Joseph Meeks and Sons of New York City were a cabinet making family. Joseph opened his New York City shop in 1789. His sons later joined the firm and helped keep the production going until 1868. Their father was a leader in the switch from some of the elaborate early Empire styles with their excessive leaf and plume carvings to a more simplified pillar and scroll Empire design. The Meeks rococo furniture emulates that made by John Belter.

Rosewood Meeks arm chair and side chair from a five-piece parlor set with carved crests. Arm chair: 24" arm to arm, 44" high. Side chair: 41" high. Middle Century.

MERIDIENNE (or Recamier)

A meridienne is a small chaise lounge (an elongated reclining chair). It can be either a left or right style, depending on where the back and side supports are located.

Mahogany stained meridienne or recaimer with fretwork at crest, 28" wide, 36" high, 4" rail, Late Century.

MUSIC BOX

A music box is a case containing a bar with tuned steel teeth that are struck by pins arranged on a revolving cylinder so as to produce a tune.

Mahogany Regina music box with 15" discs, 22" wide, 13" deep, 48" high, 4" rail, Late Century.

P

PARLOUR SUIT(E)
(or Parlor Set)

The 1876 spelling for a matching set of parlor funiture is given in the heading. Generally included are seats for more than one occupant such as a sofa, love seat for two, or a settee. Various chairs are included. There may be a matching lady's and gentleman's chair and side chairs. Sets with a larger number of pieces can have both a sofa and a love seat or settee in addition to the various chairs.

Rosewood rococo four-piece parlor set consisting of a sofa (below), an arm chair (left) and two side chairs (right) with button backs, pierced carving at crests and cabriole legs. Sofa: 68" arm to arm. Arm chair: 24" arm to arm, 39" high. Side chair: 36" high, Middle Century.

Walnut rococo five-piece parlor set consisting of an arm chair (left), a sofa (right), and three side chairs with button backs and seats and carving at crests. Sofa: 65" arm to arm. Arm chair: 28" arm to arm, 41" high. Side chair: 36" high. Middle Century.

Mahogany and mahogany stained late Empire five-piece parlor set with tufted backs, consisting of a sofa (above), rocking chair, (below left), arm chair, and two side chairs with low arms, one of which is pictured (below right). Sofa: 52" arm to arm. Rocker: 27" arm to arm. Side chair: 39" high. (Arm chair not pictured.) Late Century.

Mahogany and mahogany stained four-piece parlor set with fretwork backs consisting of a sofa, side chair (right), arm chair and a meridienne (below). Sofa: 48" arm to arm. Side chair: 39" high. Arm chair: 24" arm to arm, 39" high. Meridienne: 28" wide, 36" high. Late Century.

PEDESTAL

A pedestal table does not have legs but has a central support which can be plain or fancy and can terminate with four feet. Both wooden and marble top examples exist.

Mahogany pedestal with rope twist column, 14" square, 38" high, Late Century.

PETTICOAT MIRROR

This table with a looking glass placed in its base permitted a woman to adjust her long petticoat (underskirt) and floor-length dress. Some such mirrors were placed in the entry hall so that a skirt could be checked before a lady entered the "parlour."

Mahogany marble top petticoat mirror with paw feet and acanthus leaves design, 33" wide, 19" deep, 28" high, Early Century.

Mahogany petticoat mirror with drawer in apron and scroll feet, 45" wide, 19" deep, 35" high, Late Century.

Mahogany petticoat mirror with two drawers and scroll legs, 56" wide, 18" deep, 33" high, Late Century.

PIANO

A piano is a large stringed percussion instrument played from a keyboard.

Rosewood Chickering piano marked "Cornelius & Co., Philadelphia, 1846," 73" wide, 36" deep, 36" high, Early Century.

PIANO BENCH AND PIANO STOOL

These provided a place to sit while playing a piano. Most stool versions can be adjusted in height.

Mahogany and metal base piano stool with upholstered top, 14" diameter, Late Century.

Walnut piano bench with applied decorations, 20" wide, 15" deep, 19" high as pictured but will raise to 25", Late Century.

PIER GLASS (or Pier Mirror)

This tall, narrow mirror often hung between two long windows. Sometimes it was hung above a low wall table called a console table.

Mahogany pier mirror with pilasters at each side of glass and slanted hat mirror near top, 33" wide, 97" high, Early Century.

Walnut piano stool with octagonal upholstered top, 16" across top, height adjusts from 19" to 26", Middle Century.

PLANT STAND
A plant stand is a small table that customarily held a potted plant. These stands received their names according to the function they served, such as to hold a candle (candle- stand), music (music stand), etc.

Left photo: Walnut pier mirror with pilasters flanking mirror, applied burl veneer panels and marble top shelf, 27" wide, 13" deep, 107" high, Middle Century.

Right photo: Walnut pier mirror with applied decoration and fretwork beneath marble top shelf, 29" wide, 9" deep, 102" high, Middle Century.

Below photo: Walnut pier mirror base with marble top, whorl feet, cabriole legs and shell motif front, 33" wide, 14" deep, 20" high, Middle Century.

Mahogany Empire octagonal pedestal, 14" across top, 36" high, Early Century.

QUILT RACK

A quilt rack is a standing framework upon which quilts, stitched bedcovers made of two layers of cloth with a filling, can be displayed.

Walnut quilt or towel rack, 24" wide, 9" deep, 34" high, Late Century.

Walnut quilt or towel rack, 23" wide, 11" deep, 34" high, Late Century.

 **R**

RECAMIER (or Meridienne)

A recamier is a small chaise lounge or a reclining elongated chair that can be either left or right sided depending on where the back and side supports are located. (See Meridienne.)

RENAISSANCE REVIVAL

Renaissance furniture of the 1850-1890's represented a revival of interest in Greek and Roman culture. Elaborate carving, heavy, tall, imposing, ornamental, very ornate furniture was the norm. High bedsteads, secretary desks, and sideboards were machine made, frequently with handcarved details, including the applied game and fowls that dangled down on some sideboard door panels. Extravagant features included carved crests and pediments, applied decorations such as roundels and moldings, and the appearance of carved heads. Womanly Columbia symbolized the United States, circa 1876, the country's centenial year. George Washington's features also decorated furniture. Furniture maker John Jelliff liked to carve brave warriors and figures of women with long flowing tresses while Prudent Mallard featured females with short hair. Huge dressing cases were a part of the bedchamber suits (bedroom sets). Pedestal tables with cluttered bases abounded. Turned finials and urns were used generously. Walnut was the common wood, especially in factories, but some men chose the elite rosewood. Carved wooden pulls continued in use but ebony and gilt handles (which are now called tear drop pulls because of their shape) were prevalent also. Renaissance furniture is impressive.

Walnut Renaissance Revival marble top sideboard impressed "J. Preston" on back with burl veneer panels and applied decorations, 48" wide, 21" deep, 81" high, Middle to Late Century.

Walnut upholstered rocker with tufted back, 24" arm to arm, 40" high, Middle Century.

ROCKER (or Rocking Chair)

A rocker is a type of chair that moves backward and forward on two slightly curved runners (or rockers). A patented type may sway on a platform in some manner and is referred to as a platform rocker.

Walnut upholstered barrel back rocker with tufted back, 28" arm to arm, 37" high, Middle Century.

Walnut Louis XV Substyle upholstered rocker with finger roll and cabriole legs, 24" arm to arm, 35" high, Middle Century.

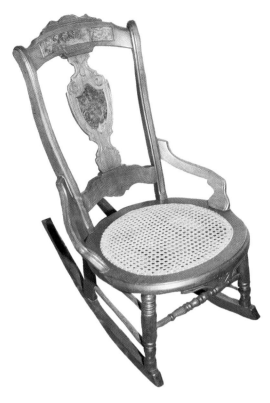

Walnut upholstered rocker with rolled arms, 24" arm to arm, 42" high, Middle to Late Century.

Walnut cane-seat rocker with burl veneer panels on splat and crest, 35" high, Late Century.

Walnut cane-seat, cane-back rocker with burl panels on crest, 33" high, Late Century.

Walnut Eastlake rocker (originally caned) with burl veneer panel on crest, 34" high, Late Century.

ROCOCO (or Louis XV Influence)

Rococo is an ornate, often asymetrical, curved style of furniture featuring rocks, shells, fruits, flowers, leaves and nuts in its designs. It was influenced by the decorative, curvaceous feminine decorations that were popular when Louis XV was France's king (1715-1774). Straight lines were avoided. Elliptical chair backs were desirable. The cabriole leg (shaped like a goat's leg) bulged at the knee, flowed in and then swelled outward at the foot. It appeared on tables, chairs, and sofas. Marble tops were common. Fruit, nut and leaf-carved handles were popular as were finger roll frames with their continuous indented valley between two gently rolling wooden ridges on chair and sofa backs. Pierced and applied (made separately and attached to a piece) carving appeared on parlor sets also. Black haircloth, a stiff fabric made from hair from the mane or tail of horses, was a common upholstery material selected. Damask (a durable, reversible, lustrous fabric with a figured weave), brocatelle (a heavy figured cloth usually made of silk and linen) and needlework completed by the women were used also. John Belter retains a leadership position in the crafting of Louis XV rococo furniture, but many feel that Prudent Mallard rates a co-leader status for his excellent work. Charles A. Baudouine and Joseph Meeks were skillful too, even though frequently their products seemed to emulate Belter's. Today, many collectors and homemakers appreciate the feminine appearance of the curved rococo furniture.

ROLL-TOP DESK

Parallel slats are a distinguishing feature of a roll-top desk. A flexible, slatted, cylindrical hood can be opened up to make the writing surface available. It can be drawn down to cover this area when the desk is not in use.

Rosewood rococo marble top server or console table with applied carving, 40" wide, 24" deep, 30" high, Middle Century.

ROPE BEDSTEAD

Instead of metal springs over slats to uphold a soft, filled ticking, ropes strung in parallel lines from pegs spaced equidistant on the wooden rails provided the base for this bed. The lacings went around the pegs from head to foot as well as crossing from side to side. The resulting webbing sagged after repeated usage, and a part of the housekeeping tasks included keeping it taut. A small, wooden, two-pronged instrument which sometimes resembled an enlarged wooden clothspin was frequently employed to twist the ropes tight. Rope bedsteads existed from the 1820's until the 1880's.

Cherry roll top, two-piece desk with S-roll made by Minneapolis Office & School Furnishing Co., patented 1882 on lock, 60" wide, 32" deep, 51" high, Late Century.

Cherry cannon ball rope bed with blanket roll on footboard, 52" wide, 59" high headboard, 37" high footboard, Early Century.

ROUX, JACQUE ALEXANDER

French-born Alexander Roux worked in New York City from the 1850's until 1881. He made high quality furniture in the prevailing styles including gothic, rococo and Renaissance. Roux used three dimensional carvings of animals and birds, including wild game dangling down on the door panels of his Renaissance sideboards. Medallions, some with a cameo appearance, were well executed. Scrolls, leaves, and fruit might be present. Some Roux labels do exist and clearly identify examples of his careful craftmanship.

Rosewood marble top table with Roux influence showing carved birds and roses, 39" wide, 31" deep, 29" high, Middle Century.

SECRETARY

A secretary is a desk usually with a bookcase above and drawers below.

SEWING STAND

A small work table that generally features a lift lid or drawers fitted with spool racks and a space for other essentials is called a sewing stand. Some had cloth bags attached or a rounded bottom drawer where fabrics or mending projects could be stored. A Martha Washington type had rounded lift-lid wooden receptables flanking the top.

Walnut cylinder front secretary with applied burl veneer panels and applied decorations, 50" wide, 24" deep, 92" high, Middle Century.

Mahogany Empire swivel sewing stand with swell front center drawers and leaf and claw feet, 23" wide, 23" deep, 31" high, Early Century.

SERVER

A server is a dining room side table that is generally higher than usual and has drawers for silverware.

Walnut server with burl veneer panels and one drawer, 56" wide, 18" deep, 33" high, Middle Century.

SHAVING STAND

Various types of stands with adjustable mirrors served as shaving stands for men. Most had a drawer where the razor and other essentials could be stored.

Mahogany marble top shaving stand, 16" wide, 15" deep top, 43" high, Early Century.

Walnut marble top ètagére sideboard with applied decorations and circular molding on drawers and doors, 58" wide, 19" deep, 90" high, Middle Century.

SIDEBOARD (or Buffet)

A sideboard is a large ornate buffet with drawers and cupboard space to hold items such as china, silver, and linens in a dining room.

Walnut marble top sideboard with applied carving and decorations, 62" wide, 29" deep, 79" high, Middle Century.

Walnut Eastlake marble top sideboard with incised lines, applied burl panels and carving, 67" wide, 24" deep, 80" high, Late Century.

Walnut Eastlake marble top sideboard with incised lines and burl veneer panels, 42" wide, 20" deep, 76" high, Late Century.

SIDELOCK

A chiffonier (tall chest of drawers) with a hinged stile (upright edge of the frame) that closes so that all drawers lock simultaneously is called a sidelock.

Walnut sidelock with burl veneer panels drawers, stiles and sides and maple and ebony inlay on top drawer, 37" wide, 24" deep, 60" high, Late Century.

Cherry projection front sidelock chest with incised lines and burl veneer drawer fronts, 29" wide, 19" deep, 45" high, Late Century.

Cherry Eastlake projection front sidelock chest with incised lines and brass rail at top, 38" wide, 20" deep, 53" high, 4" rail, Late Century.

Mahogany sidelock desk with incised lines, drop front drawer that reveals writing surface and compartments and gothic arches on top rail, 36" wide, 21" deep, 54" high, 12" rail, Middle Century.

SLIPPER CHAIR

A bedroom chair with short legs where a person could sit to remove or put on slippers or shoes with ease is called a slipper chair.

Walnut slipper chair with lift lid, tufted seat and back, applied decorations and burl veneer panels, 24" wide, 16" deep, 32" high, Late Century.

SLIPPER BENCH

A slipper bench is generally backless and has a lift lid so that slippers can be kept in the enclosed base section.

Walnut slipper bench with lift lid, 21" wide, 11" deep, 13" high, Late Century.

Walnut rococo slipper chair with pierced carving and cabriole legs, 38" high, Middle Century.

SLIP SEAT CHAIR

As the name suggests, a slip seat chair is one where the seat portion fits tightly but is not attached to the frame and can be removed readily.

Mahogany slip seat finger roll side chair with carved crest and slat, 36" high, Middle Century.

Mahogany Empire transitional sofa with tufted back, grape carved crest, carved apron and applied decorations, 78" arm to arm, 41" high, Early Century.

SOFA

A sofa is an upholstered seat with arms that accommodates more than one person.

Mahogany and feather mahogany veneer Empire sofa with a triple arch pierced carved back and applied decorations, 84" arm to arm, 40" high, Early Century.

Mahogany and mahogany veneer Empire sofa with tufted back and serpentine front, 83" wide, 39" high, Early Century.

Walnut sofa with shield back, applied burl veneer panel, decorations and serpentine front, 64" arm to arm, 39" high, Early Century.

Left photo: Mahogany Empire sofa with serpentine frame, 82" wide, 32" high, Early Century.

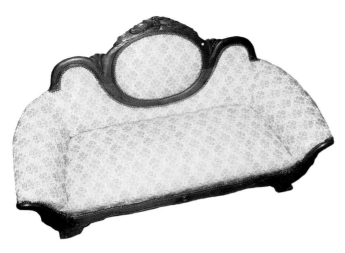

Walnut sofa with medallion back and applied carving on crest, 65" arm to arm, 32" high, Middle Century.

Rosewood sofa with tufted back, carved roses and scrolls on crest and applied decorations on molded apron, 63" arm to arm, 40" high, Middle Century.

Rosewood rococo sofa with tufted back, carved crest and apron and cabriole legs, Middle Century.

Rosewood Louis XV substyle sofa with tufted back, serpentine apron and applied carving on crest, 57" arm to arm, 42" high, Middle Century.

Walnut sofa with carved decorations on triple arches and applied burl veneer and decorations on apron, 44" arm to arm, 32" high, Middle Century.

Walnut sofa with tufted back and ornately carved frame, 59" arm to arm, 39" high, Middle Century.

Rosewood sofa with tufted back, continuous frame, decorated triple arch back, applied decorations and cabriole legs, 61" arm to arm, 40" high, Middle Century.

Rosewood sofa with triple tufted panel back, carving and applied decorations, 53" arm to arm, 43" high, Middle Century.

Walnut sofa with tufted back, pierced carving on triple arch back, applied decorations and cabriole legs, 78" arm to arm, 44" high, Middle Century.

Rosewood sofa with triple tufted panel back, cabriole legs, and flower and pierced carvings on frame, 69" arm to arm, 45" high, Middle Century.

Mahogany sofa with tufted triple medallion back, ornately carved apron and frame and cabriole legs, 66" arm to arm, 46" high, Middle Century.

Mahogany sofa with tufted back, finger roll frame and cabriole legs, 58" arm to arm, 37" high, Late Century.

Rosewood sofa with tufted back, double arch carved back, cabriole legs, and applied burl veneer on serpentine apron. 53" arm to arm, 42" high, Middle Century.

SOMNOE (or Half Commode)

Many people call a somnoe a half commode because it generally has one drawer and one door and is thus approximately half the size of an ordinary commode.

Walnut somnoe or half commode with applied burl veneer panels, 16" wide, 16" deep, 30" high, Late Century.

Walnut Eastlake sofa with tufted double framed back, incised lines, applied burl veneer panels, 58" arm to arm, 41" high, Late Century.

SPOOL CABINET

In the late 1800's and early 1900's manufacturers of thread gave display cabinets to stores. Since the company name was printed prominently on them, this served to advertise their products. Spool cabinets with several drawers in a frame now serve as holders for jewerly or scarfs. Multi-drawer units can function as end tables. Round and oval types with turning units where the spools are dispensed through a small door at the base are less common. Since these articles have been adopted to use in home decors, an example is included.

Walnut Eastlake sofa with double framed back, incised lines, applied decorations and burl veneer panels, 58" arm to arm, 38" high, Late Century.

Cherry J.P. Coats six-drawer spool cabinet, 26" wide, 20" deep, 22" high, Late Century.

STAND

Any small table used to hold or display objects such as a candle, lamp, plant, shaving materials, or music is referred to as a stand. They can be round or rectangular with oval or marble tops. A triangular type that fits into a corner is called a corner stand.

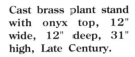

Cast brass plant stand with onyx top, 12" wide, 12" deep, 31" high, Late Century.

Mahogany and mahogany veneer Empire pedestal corner stand with scroll feet, 24" wide, 17" deep, 28" high, Early Century.

Mahogany plant stand with rope twist pedestal, 12" diameter top, 36" high, Middle to Late Century.

Mahogany plant stand with carved female figure supporting top, 13" diameter top, 36" high, Late Century.

Walnut music stand with applied burl veneer panels, lift lid and deer feet, 19" wide, 13" deep, 34" high, Middle Century.

Walnut Eastlake plant stand with incised lines, applied burl veneer panels and fretwork base, 22" wide, 16" deep, 24" high, Late Century.

Walnut sewing stand with holly and ebony inlaid star in top, incised lines and fretwork, 24" wide, 15" deep, 29" high, Late Century.

SUGAR CHEST

This is a low flat chest or a little cabinet on a stand where sugar could be stored. In the early days when sugar was expensive, a lock frequently was present. Until Civil War times (1861-1865), refined sugar was molded into loaves and cones and had to be cut with sugar shears or pulverized with a hammer before it was incorporated into a recipe. It was not until about 1870 that granulated sugar earned general acceptance.

Mahogany and mahogany veneer Empire sewing stand with sandwich glass knobs, acanthus leaf on legs and claw feet, 23" wide, 19" deep, 32" high, Early Century.

Walnut sugar chest with lift lid top and one drawer, 24" wide, 19" deep, 29" high, Middle Century.

T

TABLE

A piece of furniture with a flat, horizontal top held up by legs or a pedestal. Many forms exist and their designs tend to follow the style trends of the time period in which they were made is a table. Tables are named according to their use such as candle, center, cut-down, dining, game, lamp, library, parlor, teapoy, tilt-top, turtle top, and work.

A candle table held a candleholder. A center table was an important, larger piece that occupied a central position in the parlor. Low coffee tables, placed in front of sofas, were not made in the 1800's. Therefore, in order to provide such a table, some people currently cut down the pedestals of small Victorian examples to serve in this capacity. These are called cut-down tables. A dining table, as the name suggests, was where dinners were served. In 1850, *Godey's Magazine and Lady's Book* lauded George J. Henkels, a Philadelphia furniture maker, for his improved extension table that operated more easily than others did. Additional leaves can be pulled out or up or inserted in some manner to expand the dining surface. There are drop leaf (originally called fall leaf), round pedestal, rectangular, and other forms. Prior to the extension version's development, a series of tables had to be pushed together to accommodate numerous guests.

A game table formed a surface upon which cards or other games were played. A lamp table was designed to hold a lamp. A library table served as a site where books, magazines, and newpapers could be kept. A drawer might hold writing supplies. Parlor table was a general name for tables that served in that room. Teapoy is an archaic term for a small table that held the tea service.

Tilt-top is a table designed so that the top, hinged to a pedestal base, can be tipped to a vertical position. A turtle-top table bears a vague resemblance to the outline of a turtle. A work table is any utility table, usually with a drawer or a series of drawers. Some had drop leaves. Writing, sewing tables or bedside stands are examples.

Walnut marble top center table with ornately decorated pedestal and molded apron, 42" diameter, 30" high, Late Century.

Mahogany candle table with marble insert, 15" diameter, 33" high, Late Century.

Walnut marble top center table with ornately decorated pedestal and molded apron, 37" wide, 29" deep, 29" high, Late Century.

Walnut turtle-top center table with white marble top, applied decorations and cabriole legs, 41" wide, 30" deep, 27" high, Middle Century.

Mahogany Empire twelve-sided center table with beading on apron and scrolled legs, 35" wide, 29" high, Early Century.

Mahogany turtle-top center table with white marble top, veneered apron and applied decorations, 39" wide, 26" deep, 28" high, Middle Century.

Walnut Eastlake center table with incised lines and drop corner finials, 36" wide, 36" deep, 30" high, Late Century.

Rosewood turtle-top center table with white marble top, applied rose and magnolia carving, fretwork stretchers, 37" wide, 30" deep, 30" high, Middle Century.

Mahogany Empire center table with inlaid designs on top, apron and pedestal, 39" square, 30" high, Early Century.

Mahogany Empire center table, 34" square, 31" high, Early Century.

Walnut cut-down center table, 36" diameter, 19" high, Late Century.

Walnut cut-down marble top center table with applied decorations and molded apron, 35" wide, 23" deep, 20" high, Late Century.

Mahogamy and mahogany veneer Federal double carved pedestal dining table with three aproned leaves, 66" wide, 51" deep, 30" high, 20" leaf, Early Century.

Walnut Renaissance Revival cut-down marble top center table with applied decorations and burl veneer panels, 27" square, 23" high, Middle to Late Century.

Walnut drop leaf extension table with center support leg, 46" wide, 26" deep, 30" high, 16" drop leaf, Late Century.

850

Walnut gate leg dining table, 46" wide, 28" deep, 20" drop leaf, Late Century.

Walnut game table that can assume three positions has molded apron and cabriole legs, 34" wide, 17" deep, 28" high, Late Century.

Walnut extension split pedestal dining table with applied molded burl veneer panels and decorations and six 11" leaves, 48" diameter, 31" high, Late Century.

Walnut extension split pedestal dining table with applied molded burl veneer panels and decorations and four 11" leaves, 48" diameter, 31" high, Middle to Late Century.

Walnut lamp table with marble top, 15" diameter, 30" high, Late Century. Seen on table is John Rogers, N.Y., April 19, 1864 *Mail Day* statue.

Walnut pedestal lamp table with scalloped top and tinseled decoration under glass top, 21" diameter, 30" high, Late Century.

Walnut marble top lamp table with molded apron, 22" wide, 18" deep, 28" high, Late Century.

Walnut Renaissance Revival lamp stand with Eastlake influence, incised lines and needlepoint top, 16" diameter, 30" high, Middle to Late Century.

Walnut Eastlake marble top lamp table with incised lines, applied decorations and an identification tag found under the marble stating: "Frank B. Brown, Hampton, New Hampshire, 1886," 20" wide, 15" deep, 30" high, Late Century.

Walnut Eastlake marble (not original) top lamp table with incised lines and applied burl veneer panels, 20" wide, 18" deep, 31" high, Late Century.

Walnut lamp table with incised lines on the top and legs, 16" diameter, 30" high, Late Century.

Walnut lamp table with scalloped edge, 23" diameter, 28" high, Late Century.

Walnut lamp table with bird heads at top of leg supports, 18" diameter, 31" high, Late Century.

Walnut library table with burl veneer on drawer front and at the top of the leg supports, 42" wide, 24" deep, 30" high, Middle Century.

Mahogany marble top library table with applied decorations on drawer front and cabriole legs, 38" wide, 17" deep, 30" high, Middle Century.

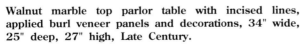

Walnut marble top parlor table with incised lines, applied burl veneer panels and decorations, 34" wide, 25" deep, 27" high, Late Century.

Center right photo: Mahogany rococo marble top parlor table with flame mahogany veneer on apron, incised lines and applied decorations, 31" wide, 18" deep, 27" high, Middle Century.

Bottom right photo: Walnut marble top parlor table with molded apron, 35" wide, 26" deep, 30" high, Late Century.

Walnut marble top parlor table with applied burl veneer on legs and apron and applied decorations, 29" wide, 21" deep, 28" high, Middle Century.

Walnut Eastlake marble top parlor table with Renaissance influence, incised lines and scribed designs, drop finials at corners and applied decorations, 28" wide, 20" deep, 30" high, Late Century.

Walnut marble top parlor table with carved pedestal and molded apron, 33" wide, 23" deep, 29" high, Middle Century.

Cherry marble top pedestal parlor table, 22" diameter, 29" high, Middle Century.

Left photo: Walnut marble top parlor table with incised lines in molded apron and applied decorations, 32" wide, 23" deep, 29" high, Late Century.

1750

Walnut Renaissance Revival turtle-top parlor table with marble top, applied burl veneer panels and decorations, 41" wide, 27" deep, 31" high, Middle to Late Century.

1500

Rosewood rococo turtle-top parlor table with marble top, carved base and applied carving on apron, 37" wide, 23" deep, 30" high, Middle Century.

750

Walnut Renaissance Revival turtle-top parlor table with marble top, molded apron, upright finials and applied decorations, 31" wide, 20" deep, 30" high, Middle to Late Century.

750

1500

Walnut turtle-top parlor table with marble top, molded apron and large leaf finial at leg juncture, 31" wide, 22" deep, 28" high, Middle to Late Century.

Left photo: Walnut turtle-top parlor table with marble top, burl veneer apron and applied decorations and cabriole legs, 38" wide, 26" deep, 30" high, Middle Century.

Walnut turtle-top parlor table with marble top and applied decorations, 30" wide, 17" deep, 28" high, Middle Century.

Walnut parlor table with molded apron and legs, 32" wide, 12" deep, 30" high, Middle to Late Century.

Walnut Renaissance Revival parlor table with cloth material insert on top, 36" wide, 24" deep, 29" high, Middle to Late Century.

Walnut parlor table with molded apron and legs, 22" wide, 18" deep, 30" high, Middle to Late Century.

Walnut Eastlake parlor table with incised lines, 30" wide, 22" deep, 29" high, Late Century.

Walnut Renaissance Revival parlor table with Eastlake influence, incised lines, molded apron, and applied decorations, 30" wide, 22" deep, 28" high, Late Century.

Walnut Renaissance Revival parlor table with marble insert, incised lines and applied burl veneer panels, 36" wide, 24" deep, 26" high, Middle to Late Century.

Walnut turtle top parlor table with molded apron and upright finial between stretchers, 32" wide, 24" deep, 28" high, Late Century.

Mahogany Federal pedestal parlor table with claw feet, 36" diameter, 29" high, Early Century. Bridal couple with a wicker wreath and feather flowers under dome.

Walnut teapoy, a small table for tea service, with one drawer, 26" wide, 18' deep, 28" high, Late Century.

106

Mahogany base turtle-top table with molded apron and carved dog on bottom shelf, 38" wide, 24" deep, 29" high, Middle Century.

Cherry work table with one drawer, 20" wide, 20" deep, 28" high, Middle Century.

Mahogany tilt-top table with inlaid designs on top and ball and claw feet, 27" diameter, 27" high when top is horizontal, Middle Century.

Walnut work table with one drawer, 21" wide, 17" deep, 29" high, Middle Century.

Cherry work table with one drawer, 21" wide, 22" deep, 30" high, Middle Century.

Cherry work table with burl veneer drawer fronts, beading around top and spool legs, 24" wide, 20" deep, 30" high, Middle Century.

Cherry work table with one drawer, 19" wide, 18" deep, 26" high, Middle Century.

Cherry work table with tiger maple drawer front, top railing and bottom shelf, 20" square, 30" high, 3" rail, Middle Century.

Cherry work table with two drawers, 21" wide, 18" deep, 29" high, Middle Century.

Cherry work table with mahogany veneer on drawer fronts, 20" wide, 17" deep, 28" high, Middle Century.

Cherry work table with two tiger maple veneered drawer fronts, 19" wide, 18" deep, 28" high, Middle Century.

Walnut and cherry work table with two drawers, 18" wide, 16" deep, 28" high, Middle Century.

Mahogany work table with three drawers, 24" wide, 17" deep, 28" high, Early Century.

Walnut drop leaf work table with burl veneered drawer fronts, 18" wide, 23" deep, 30" high, 8" leaves, Middle Century.

TESTER (or Canopy)

A tester is the roof-like framework on top of the tall posts of a four poster bed. A half tester covers the head of the bed only. Side testers also exist where the cover projects from the wall. (See Canopy Bed.)

TILT-TOP TABLE

The top of this table is hinged to a central post in its base so that it can be tipped to a vertical position.

Walnut tilt-top table with checkerboard inlay on top, 23" diameter, 29" high with top horizontal, Late Century.

TURTLE-TOP TABLE

A table that slightly resembles the outline of a turtle is called a turtle-top currently. Nelson, Matter & Co., Manufacturers of Furniture of Grand Rapids, Michigan mentioned scalloped table tops in their 1876 price list. The term "turtle" does not appear in their booklet.

Artificially grained rosewood over walnut turtle-top parlor table with marble top and applied decorations, 34" wide, 26" deep, 29" high, Middle Century.

WALL POCKET

Wall pockets were both utilitarian and decorative, and various articles could be kept in them. For example, the weekly newspaper would be near father's comfortable chair or slippers were easily available when placed in a pocket in the bed chamber.

Walnut wall pocket with incised lines and applied carving of woman's head, 17" wide, 23" high, Late Century.

Walnut wall pocket with fretwork back and applied carvings, 18" wide, 7" deep, 33" high, Late Century.

WARDROBE (or Armoire)

A big cupboard with hanging space, and perhaps a few drawers, served as a storage unit for clothes in the days before closets were built into homes. These wardrobes frequently can be taken apart for ease in transporting. They might be too large to haul upstairs or to take around corners otherwise. These types are called knock-down wardrobes.

Bottom right photo: Walnut two door wardrobe, 59" wide, 19" deep, 79" high, Middle Century.

Walnut two door wardrobe with veneered door panels, 47" wide, 16" deep, 81" high, Middle Century.

WASHSTAND

Washstands were a place for personal cleansing in the days before water was piped into houses. Water had to be carried in from the pump or the well. There were various types of washstands available. The common variety was a table with a drawer and perhaps towel bar ends. The commode washstand had a combination of drawers and cupboard space for the bowls, pitchers, soap holders, towels, and other articles. There was also a somnoe with one drawer and door that is today termed a half commode. The bureau washstand is a small chest of drawers.

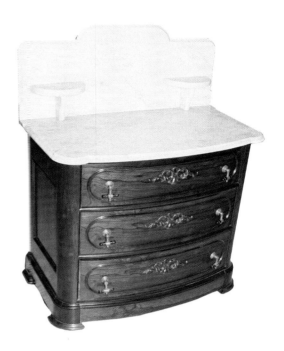

Rosewood bureau marble top washstand with splash back and soap or candlestands, bow front, applied ring molding and carved escutcheons, 34" wide, 19" deep, 30" high, 15" splash back, Middle Century.

Walnut bureau washstand with splash back and candlestands, 31" wide, 16' deep, 29" high, 11" splash back, Late Century.

Walnut bureau washstand with towel bar ends and scalloped splash back, 38" wide, 16" deep, 31" high, Late Century.

Cherry marble top commode washstand with towel bar ends and wooden splash back (not original), 40" wide, 18" deep, 30" high, 12" splash back, Middle Century.

Walnut marble top commode washstand with splash back and soap or candlestands and applied ring molding, 28" wide, 16" deep, 24" high, 12" splash back, Middle Century.

Burl walnut veneered marble top commode washstand, 35" wide, 18" deep, 31" high, Late Century.

Walnut marble top commode washstand with splash back and corner soap or candlestands and burl veneer on drawer and door panels, 31" wide, 17" deep, 30" high, 10" splash back, Late Century.

Bottom right photo: Rosewood marble top commode washstand with splash back and soap or candle stands and applied ring molding, 32" wide, 19" deep, 30" high, 12" splash back, Early Century.

Walnut marble top commode washstand with splash back and soap or candlestands and applied burl veneer panels, 29" wide, 16" deep, 30" high, 10" splash back, Late Century.

Walnut marble top commode washstand with splash back and attached Eastlake mirror with candlestands, incised lines, carving and applied burl veneer panels, 34" wide, 18" deep, 78" high, Late Century.

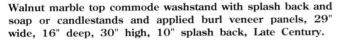

Walnut marble top commode washstand with splash back, burl veneer front panels, 36" wide, 18" deep, 28" high, 10" splash back, Late Century.

Walnut Eastlake marble top commode washstand with splash back and incised lines, 27" wide, 15" deep, 28" high, 5" splash back, Late Century.

Cherry commode washstand, 31" wide, 18" deep, 31" high, Middle Century.

Mahogany rococo commode washstand with swing bevel mirror and applied decorations, 42" wide, 20" deep, 72" high, Middle Century.

Cherry commode washstand with towel bar at back, 35" wide, 19" deep, 28" high, Late Century.

Walnut commode washstand with splash back and candle-stands, applied decorations and ring molding on drawer and doors, 30" wide, 16" deep, 32" high, 9" splash back, Late Century.

Walnut half commode washstand or somnoe with applied burl veneer panels and decorations, 23" wide, 14" deep, 36" high, Late Century.

Walnut half commode washstand or somnoe with applied ring molding, 18" wide, 18" deep, 32" high, Late Century.

Walnut marble top (not original) half commode washstand or somnoe with mirror back and burl veneer on drawer and door, 18" wide, 15" deep, 31" high, 13" mirror back, Late Century.

Cherry washstand with one drawer and hole in top for wash basin, 16" wide, 16" deep, 28" high, Middle Century.

Mahogany marble top half commode washstand or somnoe with burl veneer, applied decorations and ring molding, 18" wide, 18" deep, 3_" high, Middle Century.

Walnut half commode washstand with burl veneer panels on door and stiles, 18" wide, 16" deep, 31" high, Late Century.

Walnut washstand with marble top and spool legs, 32" wide, 18" deep, 29" high, 7" splash back, Middle Century.

WHATNOT (or Ètagére)

A whatnot is a tier of shelves connected by turned posts used to display curios. Many stand flat against the wall while some are triangular and stand in corners. Fancy versions are called étagères.

Walnut washstand, 28" wide, 17" deep, 29" high, 4" splash back, Late Century.

Walnut common washstand with towel bar ends, 29" bar to bar, 16" deep, 29" high, 4" splash back, Late Century.

Walnut five shelf wall whatnot with fretwork backs, 29" wide at base, 21" wide at top, 9" deep at base, 5" deep at top, 53" high, Late Century.

Walnut and burl walnut three shelf wall whatnot with fretwork backs, 32" wide, 16" deep, 48" high, Late Century.

WIG VANITY

A vanity where a person sat to take care of his or her artificial hair piece or to see that it was placed on the head properly. Objects such as a small wig bellows that blew out dirt or insects could be placed on top of the table as well as other implements needed for caring for the hair.

Crotch walnut veneer wig vanity with a storage compartment on each side of mirror, 42" wide, 19" deep, 62" high, Early Century.

WORK TABLE

Utility tables were called work tables. Examples include sewing stands where women kept their needlework supplies and mending; small tables where correspondence could be answered; or bedside tables. Usually the table had one or more drawers.

Walnut six shelf corner whatnot with fretwork backs, 28" wide at base, 14" wide at top, 19" deep at base, 9" deep at top, 64" high, Late Century.

Walnut drop leaf work table with two drawers, 20" wide, 24" deep, 29" high, 11" drops, Middle Century.

Y

YOUTH BED

This is an intermediate size bed between a baby and an adult version. Some have low side guard rails.

Walnut youth bed, 52" wide, 22" deep, 36" high, Late Century.

Walnut Eastlake youth bed with incised lines and applied burl veneer panels, 41" wide, 60" high headboard, 30" high footboard, Late Century.

BIBLIOGRAPHY

Aronson, Joseph. *The Encyclopedia of Furniture.*
New York, NY: Crown Publishers, Inc., 1965.

Bradford, Ernle. *Dictionary of Antiques.*
London, England: The English Universities Press Ltd., 1963.

Cowie, Donald and Keith Henshaw. *Antique Collector's Dictionary.*
New York, NY: Gramercy Publishing Company, 1962.

Meyer, Priscilla S. *Victorian Dictionary.*
Armonk, NY: Oak Cottage Farm, 1980.

Nelson, Matter & Co., Catalogue, *Manufacturers of Furniture.*
Grand Rapids, MI, January 1st, 1873.

Nelson, Matter & Co., Catalogue, *Manufacturers of Furniture.*
Grand Rapids, MI, March, 1876.

Shull, Thelma. *Victorian Antiques.*
Rutland, VT: Charles E. Tuttle Company, 1963.

Swedberg, Robert and Harriett. *Victorian Furniture Styles and Prices, Book I Revised.* West Des Moines, IA: Wallace-Homestead Book Co., 1984.

Swedberg, Robert and Harriett. *Victorian Furniture Styles and Prices, Book II Revised.* Des Moines, IA: Wallace-Homestead Book Co., 1983.

Swedberg, Robert and Harriett. *Victorian Furniture Styles and Prices, Book III.* Radnor, PA: Wallace-Homestead Book Co., 1985.

PRICE GUIDE

Pages 8-9

Armoire ....$ 895.00
Banquet table 1,295.00
Bedroom set 7,500.00

Pages 10-11

2 pc. Renaissance Revival
   bedroom set, Jelliff influenced 7,500.00
2 pc. Renaissance Revival bedroom set.......6,500.00
3 pc. Renaissance Revival bedroom set.......7,500.00

Pages 12-13

4 pc. Renaissance Revival bedroom set.......4,500.00
2 pc. bedroom set, Middle Century 7,500.00
2 pc. bedroom set, Late Century.................1,275.00

Pages 14-15

3 pc. Eastlake bedroom set 2,400.00
3 pc. Renaissance Revival bedroom set.......3,995.00
2 pc. Eastlake bedroom set 4,000.00

Pages 16-17

4 pc. bedroom set..6,000.00
Four poster rope bed 2,500.00
Eastlake half-tester bed 3,000.00
Mahogany half-tester bed 7,000.00
Bedstead headboard 725.00

Pages 18-19

Bedstead, applied decorations 475.00
Bedstead headboard 3,500.00
Bedstead, striped veneer 3,750.00
Rope bedstead, blanket rail............................650.00
Henry Clay side chair 1,500.00
Rosalie side chair 2,000.00

Pages 20-21

Eastlake single door bookcase,
   spoon carving......................................975.00
Double door bookcase 1,950.00
Eastlake single door bookcase 990.00
Renaissance Revival buffet 3,000.00
Bureau 2,250.00
Bureau washstand 335.00
Butler's desk 1,800.00

Pages 22-23

Curio cabinet..700.00
Barber's cabinet..475.00
Eastlake dental cabinet 1,500.00

Dental cabinet $6,500.00
Candlestand 250.00
Canopy bedstead 5,550.00
Canterbury 175.00

Pages 24-25

Canterbury 950.00
Pedestal game table 700.00
Center table..1,200.00
Chippendale arm chair....................................875.00
Arm chair, open arms, cabriole legs 600.00
Arm chair, tufted back..................................1,500.00
Arm chair, dolphin arm supports 1,250.00

Pages 26-27

Jelliff influenced arm chair............................450.00
Eastlake arm chair, tufted back 195.00
Eastlake arm chair..159.00
Cane-seat arm chair..250.00
Eastlake cane-seat and back arm chair 250.00
Rosalie side chair 3,750.00
Pressed cane kitchen chair..............................225.00
Cane-seat chair, flat front rung 55.00

Pages 28-29

Cane-seat chair ....Set of six 1,500.00
Cane-seat chair, balloon back....Set of five   650.00
Cane-seat chair, burl veneer
   decorations ....Set of six   750.00
Eastlake cane-seat and back chair..................285.00
Cane-seat chair 130.00
Eastlake cane-seat tilt back office chair 750.00
Gentleman's chair, open arms, tufted back ...800.00
Gentleman's chair, carved crest 1,850.00

Pages 30-31

Lady's chair, Louis XV substyle,
   tufted back 600.00
Eastlake transitional lady's chair....................475.00
Renaissance Revival lady's chair 125.00
Lady's chair, Louis XV substyle......................475.00
Louis XV lady's and gentleman's
   matching chairs, horsehair upholstery 1,200.00
Louis XV lady's and gentleman's
   matching chairs 2,250.00

Pages 32-33

Louis XV matching lady's and gentleman's
   (beige colored set) 1,400.00

Louis XV matching lady's and
   gentleman's chairs (rose colored set) .....$ 595.00
Photographer's chair 350.00
Side chair, applied carved crest, slip seat 135.00
Empire side chair, veneered 200.00
Empire side chair, walnut burl 275.00
Empire side chair, carved crest 200.00

Pages 34-35

Empire side chair, lyre splat 225.00
Side chair, C-scroll, carved roses 600.00
Louis XV rococo side chair, fruit C-scroll 600.00
Louis XV rococo side chair,
   carved morning glory, grapes, leaves 650.00
Louis XV side chair,
   tufted back ....Set of six   3,100.00
Louis XV rococo side chair 500.00
Side chair, carved roses 175.00
Rococo side chair..1,500.00

Pages 36-37

Louis XV substyle side chair,
   carved and pieced crest 175.00
Louis XV substyle balloon back side chair ...265.00
Side chair, originally caned...........................115.00
Renaissance Revival side chair,
   Eastlake influenced, burl veneer 500.00
Eastlake side chair 170.00
Renaissance Revival side chair
   Eastlake influence, tufted back 150.00
Eastlake side chair 125.00
Sidelock chest...1,200.00

Pages 38-39

Chiffonier 1,750.00
China cabinet 2,700.00
Commode washstand......................................475.00
Common washstand...225.00
Corner cupboard,
   Early Century or late 1700's 8,500.00
Corner cupboard,
   Middle Century 1,750.00
Corner cupboard,
   90" high, Middle Century 2,250.00
Corner cupboard,
   Middle Century, 76" high 1,250.00

Pages 40-41

Corner cupboard, one drawer 2,000.00
Cradle, on rockers 295.00
Cradle, swings on frame................................1,250.00
2 pc. closed cupboard, Early Century 2,200.00
2 pc. closed cupboard, Middle Century 1,650.00
2 pc. step-back cupboard,
   cherry and mahogany 950.00
2 pc. step-back cupboard, cherry................1,250.00
2 pc. step-back cupboard, walnut..................975.00

Pages 42-43

Cupboard, walnut $1,500.00
Cylinder front secretary 2,500.00
Davenport desk 1,500.00
Day bed, blanket roll ends 325.00
Day bed 300.00
Butler's desk 1,350.00

Pages 44-45

Empire butler's secretary 1,000.00
Cylinder front desk 2,000.00
Cylinder front secretary, 95" high 3,500.00
Cylinder front secretary, 92" high 1,750.00
Eastlake cylinder front secretary 2,350.00
Eastlake drop front parlor desk,
   marble top 1,800.00
Eastlake drop front parlor desk 1,250.00
Eastlake lift top davenport desk 1,550.00

Pages 46-47

Eastlake drop front secretary 2,000.00
Renaissance Revival bookcase secretary 3,500.00
Knee hole desk 1,200.00
Drop front table desk 695.00
Slant front secretary 2,000.00
Empire secretary 2,890.00
Slant front desk 2,500.00

Pages 48-49

Slant front desk 3,000.00
Slant front secretary 2,500.00
Empire whatnot desk 1,750.00
11 pc. dining room set 6,500.00
Chest on frame...8,500.00

Pages 50-51

Empire dresser, scroll feet.............................310.00
Empire dresser, scalloped 525.00
Empire dresser, cherry 675.00
Empire projection front dresser 650.00
Projection front dresser 425.00
Ètagére rococo marble top dresser.............3,000.00
Dresser with decks..350.00
Renaissance Revival dresser 850.00

Pages 52-53

Marble top dresser 1,850.00
Empire marble top dresser 2,000.00
Marble top dresser, feather veneered 1,200.00
Marble top dresser, swing mirror, decks 950.00
Marble insert dresser.....................................995.00
Marble top dresser, secret drawer in base ...895.00
Marble top dresser, swing mirror, boxes 700.00
Marble top dresser, fretwork on mirror.........950.00

Pages 54-55

Renaissance Revival cheval dresser.............2,500.00

Marble top Rococo dresser $1,850.00
Wig dresser, marble insert 2,200.00
Marble top wig dresser 575.00
Dresser, wishbone mirror 675.00
Projection front dresser 900.00
Dresser, with decks..........................425.00
Dressing table..............................4,000.00

Pages 56-57
Dry sink......................................2,500.00
Easel, carved leaf and grape finial 600.00
Easel, carved 600.00
Eastlake drop front parlor desk 1,250.00

Pages 58-59
Empire dresser 425.00
Full-length mirror ètagére 4,500.00
Ètagére, marble top, fretwork pediment 2,250.00
Full-length mirror ètagére, marble top 4,500.00
Rosewood ètagére, drawer at base..............1,850.00
Walnut ètagére, applied decorations 2,200.00
Walnut ètagére with half mirror 3,500.00

Pages 60-61
Marble top ètagére, ornate carvings 7,500.00
Marble top ètagére, fretwork pediment.......8,000.00
Ètagére, rosewood graining 2,500.00
Marble top ètagére, bow front drawer
   over circular door..............................6,500.00
Ètagére, burl veneer facing..........................1,575.00
Corner ètagére....................................2,500.00
Fireplace mantel 1,000.00
Fireplace screen 500.00

Pages 62-63
Fireside rocker 450.00
Empire footstool 150.00
Footstool, cabriole legs 150.00
Footstool, molded apron and legs 275.00
Double roll footstool................................150.00
Game table, ogee apron 550.00
Game table, blue felt insert 1,250.00
Game table, checkerboard top 450.00

Pages 64-65
Gothic child's chair................................350.00
Louis XV grandfather's chair 1,500.00
Marble top half commode 750.00
Half-tester bedstead 3,600.00
Walnut hall tree 1,950.00

Pages 66-67
Hall tree, eight turned hat holders 725.00
Hall tree, seven turned hat holders 1,000.00
Renaissance Revival hall tree 1,250.00
Hanging cupboard 350.00
Hunzinger rocker 350.00

Pages 68-69
Jelliff master or grandfather's chair $1,200.00
Jelly cupboard, molded panels 1,195.00
Jelly cupboard....................................495.00
Knee hole desk 2,500.00
Marble top lamp table 450.00

Pages 70-71
Lift top commode, 2 doors 425.00
Renaissance Revival library table 400.00
Lift top commode, 1 drawer, 2 doors 350.00
Lift top commode, towel bar ends 475.00
Louis XV medallion back sofa......................1,200.00

Pages 72-73
Marble top dressing table 3,500.00
Medallion sofa 950.00
Meeks arm chair..................................10,000.00
Meridienne 675.00
Regina music box 15,000.00

Pages 74-75
Rococo 4 pc. parlor set 10,000.00
Rococo 5 pc. parlor set 6,500.00

Pages 76-77
Empire 5 pc. parlor set 4,800.00
4 pc. parlor set..................................2,495.00
Pedestal..600.00
Marble top petticoat mirror 1,200.00

Pages 78-79
Petticoat mirror, drawer in apron 700.00
Petticoat mirror, two drawers 600.00
Chickering piano 3,000.00
Piano bench 400.00
Piano stool, octagonal top 295.00
Piano stool, metal base 65.00
Pier mirror with pilasters 1,200.00

Pages 80-81
Pier mirror, with pilasters 1,200.00
Pier mirror, applied decorations, fretwork ..1,200.00
Pier mirror base with marble top..................300.00
Empire octagonal pedestal 350.00
Quilt or towel rack, 24" wide 250.00
Quilt or towel rack, 23" wide 210.00

Pages 82-83
Renaissance Revival sideboard 3,000.00
Barrel back rocker..................................600.00
Upholstered rocker, tufted back 450.00
Louis XV upholstered rocker......................585.00
Upholstered rocker, rolled arms 595.00
Cane-seat and back rocker..........................165.00
Cane-seat rocker..................................200.00
Eastlake rocker....................................270.00

Pages 84-85

Rococo marble top server $2,500.00
Roll top, 2 pc. desk 2,000.00
Cannon ball rope bed 900.00
Marble top table, Roux influenced 7,000.00

Pages 86-87

Cylinder front secretary 2,200.00
Server, burl veneer panels 1,850.00
Empire swivel sewing stand 450.00
Marble top shaving stand.......................850.00
Marble top sideboard ....No Price Available
Marble top ètagére sideboard 3,500.00
Eastlake marble top sideboard 1,400.00

Pages 88-89

Eastlake marble top sideboard 1,250.00
Projection front sidelock chest 1,200.00
Sidelock, burl veneer panels.......................2,500.00
Eastlake projection front sidelock 1,075.00
Sidelock desk 2,000.00
Slipper bench 175.00
Slipper chair 750.00
Rococo slipper chair 875.00

Pages 90-91

Slip seat finger roll side chair 175.00
Empire sofa, tufted back 1,950.00
Empire sofa, serpentine frame 795.00
Empire transitional sofa 1,200.00
Empire sofa, triple arch back 3,500.00
Sofa, shield back 295.00
Sofa, medallion back 795.00
Rococo sofa 9,500.00
Sofa, triple arches, walnut 1,100.00
Sofa, tufted back, carved roses 3,500.00
Louis XV substyle sofa 2,000.00
Sofa, ornately carved frame 3,500.00

Pages 92-93

Sofa, continuous frame, triple arch back 2,800.00
Sofa, tufted back, triple arch back 3,000.00
Sofa, tufted triple medallion back 6,500.00
Sofa, triple tufted panel back.....................4,500.00
Sofa, flower and pierced carvings.................5,000.00
Sofa, finger roll frame, cabriole legs.............1,100.00
Sofa, double arch carved back 2,500.00
Eastlake sofa, 41" high 450.00
Eastlake sofa, 38" high 195.00
Somnoe 550.00
J.P. Coats 6-drawer spool cabinet 750.00

Pages 94-95

Empire pedestal corner stand 700.00
Music stand..450.00
Cast brass plant stand 650.00

Plant stand, rope twist pedestal..................$ 700.00
Plant stand, carved female figure 700.00
Sewing stand 790.00
Empire sewing stand 2,000.00
Eastlake plant stand 250.00
Sugar chest 1,150.00

Pages 96-97

Candle table 350.00
Marble top center table, 42" diameter..........4,500.00
Marble top center table, 37" wide 2,000.00
Turtle top center table 41" wide 1,850.00
Turtle top center table, 39" wide 1,850.00
Turtle top center table,
    applied rose, magnolia carving 6,500.00
Empire 12-sided center table 675.00
Eastlake center table 425.00
Empire center table, inlaid designs 2,500.00

Pages 98-99

Empire center table, 34" square 650.00
Cut-down marble top center table 900.00
Renaissance Revival cut-down
    marble top center table 550.00
Cut-down center table, 36" diameter 250.00
Federal pedestal dining table 5,700.00
Drop leaf extension table 700.00
Gate leg dining table..............................850.00
Extension split pedestal dining table,
    six 11" leaves 4,500.00
Extension split pedestal dining table,
    four 11" leaves 1,850.00
Game table 400.00
Lamp table 400.00

Pages 100-101

Pedestal lamp table...............................300.00
Renaissance Revival lamp stand 390.00
Marble top lamp table 450.00
Eastlake marble top lamp table 350.00
Eastlake marble (not original) top table 275.00
Lamp table, scalloped edge......................225.00
Lamp table, incised lines on top and legs.....200.00
Lamp table, bird heads on leg supports 135.00

Pages 102-103

Library table.....................................365.00
Marble top parlor table...........................950.00
Marble top library table 1,200.00
Rococo marble top parlor table....................650.00
Marble top parlor table, molded apron 750.00
Marble top parlor table, 29" wide 950.00
Marble top parlor table, 33" wide 1,850.00
Marble top parlor table, 32" wide 1,200.00
Eastlake marble top parlor table 550.00
Marble top pedestal parlor table, 22" 225.00

Schroeder's Antiques Price Guide

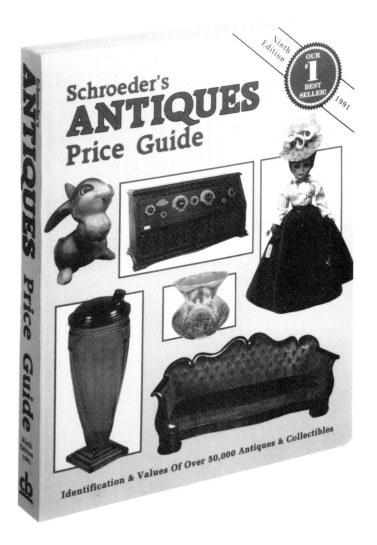

Schroeder's Antiques Price Guide has climbed its way to the top in a field already supplied with several well-established publications! The word is out, *Schroeder's Price Guide* is the best buy at any price. Over 500 categories are covered, with more than 50,000 listings. But it's not volume alone that makes Schroeder's the unique guide it is recognized to be. From ABC Plates to Zsolnay, if it merits the interest of today's collector, you'll find it in Schroeder's. Each subject is represented with histories and background information. In addition, hundreds of sharp original photos are used each year to illustrate not only the rare and the unusual, but the everyday "fun-type" collectibles as well -- not postage stamp pictures, but large close-up shots that show important details clearly.

Each edition is completely re-typeset from all new sources. We have not and will not simply change prices in each new edition. All new copy and all new illustrations make Schroeder's THE price guide on antiques and collectibles.

The writing and researching team behind this giant is proportionately large. It is backed by a staff of more than seventy of Collector Books' finest authors, as well as a board of advisors made up of well-known antique authorities and the country's top dealers, all specialists in their fields. Accuracy is their primary aim. Prices are gathered over the entire year previous to publication, from ads and personal contacts. Then each category is thoroughly checked to spot inconsistencies, listings that may not be entirely reflective of actual market dealings, and lines too vague to be of merit.

Only the best of the lot remains for publication. You'll find *Schroeder's Antiques Price Guide* the one to buy for factual information and quality.

No dealer, collector or investor can afford not to own this book. It is available from your favorite bookseller or antiques dealer at the low price of $12.95. If you are unable to find this price guide in your area, it's available from Collector Books, P. O. Box 3009, Paducah, KY 42001 at $12.95 plus $2.00 for postage and handling.

8½ x 11, 608 Pages $12.95

COLLECTOR BOOKS
A Division of Schroeder Publishing Co., Inc.

Books on Antiques and Collectibles

Most of the following books are available from your local book seller or antique dealer, or on loan from your public library. If you are unable to locate certain titles in your area you may order by mail from COLLECTOR BOOKS, P.O. Box 3009, Paducah, KY 42002-3009. Add $2.00 for postage for the first book ordered and $.25 for each additional book. Include item number, title and price when ordering. Allow 14 to 21 days for delivery. All books are well illustrated and contain current values.

Books on Glass and Pottery

1810	American Art Glass, Shuman	$29.95
1517	American Belleek, Gaston	$19.95
2016	Bedroom & Bathroom Glassware of the Depression Years	$19.95
1312	Blue & White Stoneware, McNerney	$9.95
1959	Blue Willow, 2nd Ed., Gaston	$14.95
1627	Children's Glass Dishes, China & Furniture II, Lechler	$19.95
1892	Collecting Royal Haeger, Garmon	$19.95
2017	Collector's Ency. of Depression Glass, Florence, 9th Ed.	$19.95
1373	Collector's Ency of Amercian Dinnerware, Cunningham	$24.95
1812	Collector's Ency. of Fiesta, Huxford	$19.95
1439	Collector's Ency. of Flow Blue China, Gaston	$19.95
1961	Collector's Ency of Fry Glass, Fry Glass Society	$24.95
1813	Collector's Encyclopedia of Geisha Girl Porcelain, Litts	$19.95
1664	Collector's Ency. of Heisey Glass, Bredehoft	$24.95
1915	Collector's Ency. of Hall China, 2nd Ed., Whitmyer	$19.95
1358	Collector's Ency. of McCoy Pottery, Huxford	$19.95
1039	Collector's Ency. of Nippon Porcelain I, Van Patten	$19.95
1350	Collector's Ency. of Nippon Porcelain II, Van Patten	$19.95
1665	Collector's Ency. of Nippon Porcelain III, Van Patten	$24.95
1447	Collector's Ency. of Noritake, Van Patten	$19.95
1038	Collector's Ency. of Occupied Japan, 2nd Ed., Florence	$14.95
1719	Collector's Ency. of Occupied Japan III, Florence	$19.95
2019	Collector's Ency. of Occupied Japan IV, Florence	$14.95
1715	Collector's Ency. of R.S. Prussia II, Gaston	$24.95
1034	Collector's Ency. of Roseville Pottery, Huxford	$19.95
1035	Collector's Ency. of Roseville Pottery, 2nd Ed., Huxford	$19.95
1623	Coll. Guide to Country Stoneware & Pottery, Raycraft	$9.95
1523	Colors in Cambridge, National Cambridge Society	$19.95
1425	Cookie Jars, Westfall	$9.95
1843	Covered Animal Dishes, Grist	$14.95
1844	Elegant Glassware of the Depression Era, 3rd Ed., Florence	$19.95
2024	Kitchen Glassware of the Depression Years, 4th Florence	$19.95
1465	Haviland Collectibles & Art Objects, Gaston	$19.95
1917	Head Vases Id & Value Guide, Cole	$14.95
1392	Majolica Pottery, Katz-Marks	$9.95
1669	Majolica Pottery, 2nd Series, Katz-Marks	$9.95
1919	Pocket Guide to Depression Glass, 6th Ed., Florence	$9.95
1438	Oil Lamps II, Thuro	$19.95
1670	Red Wing Collectibles, DePasquale	$9.95
1440	Red Wing Stoneware, DePasquale	$9.95
1958	So. Potteries Blue Ridge Dinnerware, 3rd Ed., Newbound	$14.95
1889	Standard Carnival Glass, 2nd Ed., Edwards	$24.95
1941	Standard Carnival Glass Price Guide, Edwards	$7.95
1814	Wave Crest, Glass of C.F. Monroe, Cohen	$29.95
1848	Very Rare Glassware of the Depression Years, Florence	$24.95

Books on Dolls & Toys

1887	American Rag Dolls, Patino	$14.95
1749	Black Dolls, Gibbs	$14.95
1514	Character Toys & Collectibles 1st Series, Longest	$19.95
1750	Character Toys & Collectibles, 2nd Series, Longest	$19.95
2021	Collectible Male Action Figures, Manos	$14.95
1529	Collector's Ency. of Barbie Dolls, DeWein	$19.95
1066	Collector's Ency. of Half Dolls, Marion	$29.95
1891	French Dolls in Color, 3rd Series, Smith	$14.95
1631	German Dolls, Smith	$9.95
1635	Horsman Dolls, Gibbs	$19.95
1067	Madame Alexander Collector's Dolls, Smith	$19.95
2025	Madame Alexander Price Guide #15, Smith	$7.95
1995	Modern Collectors Dolls, Vol. I, Smith	$19.95

1516	Modern Collector's Dolls V, Smith	$19.95
1540	Modern Toys, 1930-1980, Baker	$19.95
2033	Patricia Smith Doll Values, Antique to Modern, 6th ed.,	$9.95
1886	Stern's Guide to Disney	$14.95
1513	Teddy Bears & Steiff Animals, Mandel	$9.95
1817	Teddy Bears & Steiff Animals, 2nd, Mandel	$19.95
2028	Toys, Antique & Collectible, Longest	$14.95
1630	Vogue, Ginny Dolls, Smith	$19.95
1648	World of Alexander-Kins, Smith	$19.95
1808	Wonder of Barbie, Manos	$9.95
1430	World of Barbie Dolls, Manos	$9.95

Other Collectibles

1457	American Oak Furniture, McNerney	$9.95
1846	Antique & Collectible Marbles, Grist, 2nd Ed.	$9.95
1712	Antique & Collectible Thimbles, Mathis	$19.95
1880	Antique Iron, McNerney	$9.95
1748	Antique Purses, Holiner	$19.95
1868	Antique Tools, Our American Heritage, McNerney	$9.95
2015	Archaic Indian Points & Knives, Edler	$14.95
1426	Arrowheads & Projectile Points, Hothem	$7.95
1278	Art Nouveau & Art Deco Jewelry, Baker	$9.95
1714	Black Collectibles, Gibbs	$19.95
1666	Book of Country, Raycraft	$19.95
1960	Book of Country Vol II, Raycraft	$19.95
1811	Book of Moxie, Potter	$29.95
1128	Bottle Pricing Guide, 3rd Ed., Cleveland	$7.95
1751	Christmas Collectibles, Whitmyer	$19.95
1752	Christmas Ornaments, Johnston	$19.95
1713	Collecting Barber Bottles, Holiner	$24.95
2018	Collector's Ency. of Graniteware, Greguire	$24.95
1634	Coll. Ency. of Salt & Pepper Shakers, Davern	$19.95
2020	Collector's Ency. of Salt & Pepper Shakers II, Davern	$19.95
1916	Collector's Guide to Art Deco, Gaston	$14.95
1753	Collector's Guide to Baseball Memorabilia, Raycraft	$14.95
1537	Collector's Guide to Country Baskets, Raycraft	$9.95
1437	Collector's Guide to Country Furniture, Raycraft	$9.95
1842	Collector's Guide to Country Furniture II, Raycraft	$14.95
1962	Collector's Guide to Decoys, Huxford	$14.95
1441	Collector's Guide to Post Cards, Wood	$9.95
1716	Fifty Years of Fashion Jewelry, Baker	$19.95
2022	Flea Market Trader, 6th Ed., Huxford	$9.95
1668	Flint Blades & Proj. Points of the No. Am. Indian, Tully	$24.95
1755	Furniture of the Depression Era, Swedberg	$19.95
1424	Hatpins & Hatpin Holders, Baker	$9.95
1964	Indian Axes & Related Stone Artifacts, Hothem	$14.95
2023	Keen Kutter Collectibles, Heuring	$14.95
1212	Marketplace Guide to Oak Furniture, Blundell	$17.95
1918	Modern Guns, Id. & Values, 7th Ed., Quertermous	$12.95
1181	100 Years of Collectible Jewelry, Baker	$9.95
1965	Pine Furniture, Our Am. Heritage, McNerney	$14.95
1124	Primitives, Our American Heritage, McNerney	$8.95
1759	Primitives, Our American Heritage, 2nd Series, McNerney	$14.95
2026	Railroad Collectibles, 4th Ed., Baker	$14.95
1632	Salt & Pepper Shakers, Guarnaccia	$9.95
1888	Salt & Pepper Shakers II, Guarnaccia	$14.95
1816	Silverplated Flatware, 3rd Ed., Hagan	$14.95
2027	Standard Baseball Card Pr. Gd., Florence	$9.95
1922	Standard Bottle Pr. Gd., Sellari	$14.95
1966	Standard Fine Art Value Guide, Huxford	$29.95
1890	The Old Book Value Guide	$19.95
1923	Wanted to Buy	$9.95
1885	Victorian Furniture, McNerney	$9.95